*The
Divine
Triunity*

*The
Divine
Triunity*

by Norman Pittenger

*A Pilgrim Book
from
United Church Press
Philadelphia*

Library of Congress Cataloging in Publication Data
Pittenger, William Norman, 1905–
    The divine triunity.

    "A Pilgrim book."
    Bibliography: p.
    1. Trinity.   2. Process theology.   I. Title.
BT111.2.P57   231   76-55002
ISBN 0-8298-0330-0

United Church Press,
1505 Race Street, Philadelphia, Pennsylvania 19102

For
James A. Carpenter,
former student of mine, learned
scholar, and now professor of theology
at the General Seminary in New York,
whose insistent urging that I write a
book on the doctrine of the Trinity
has led me to produce this volume

Contents

Preface

In an age when we are much con-
cerned with the effort to "reconceive" the basic affirmations of Christian faith, the doctrine of the Trinity—God as
"three in one and one in three"—seems to many to be one
aspect of that inherited tradition which has little if anything
to say to us today. The doctrine, with its talk of threeness and
oneness, appears to be either a mathematical absurdity (for
how can three be one and one three?) or else one of those
supposed "mysteries" about which the less said the better. In
any event, what practical meaning can it have, how can it be
relevant to the Christian life as people must live it today, and
in what fashion can we claim, as the historical theological
formulations have always dared to do, that the "triunity of
God" is essential to a full-orbed and adequate understanding
of deity in relationship with humankind?

It may be worth observing that I have
just spoken of the "triunity," rather than the "trinity"; and I
am convinced that this terminology is important. To talk of
"trinity" may very well suggest to some a tritheistic view of
God—God the Father, God the Son or Word, and God the
Spirit—which would be the contradiction of the essential
monotheism, the doctrine that there is but *one* God, which is
fundamental to the entire Jewish-Christian development of
religious insight, understanding, and interpretation. But to
say "triunity" is to speak of oneness *and* threeness; it is to
point toward a rich complexity and fullness in the divine na-

ture, a nature about which we can have, at best, only intimations and indications. I for one am convinced that this is the right way to talk about God, and I hope that this book will help to show why I hold this view. God is both social and personal, both rich in relationship and yet fully personalized; so, I believe, both the tradition we inherit and the experience we share will tell us.

One of the difficulties facing a theologian today is the language which is to be employed in speaking of God. In attempting to meet this problem in the present book, I have felt both the inadequacy of the masculine pronoun *and* the danger of suggesting, by use of some other idiom, an impersonal conception of deity. Hence I have used the traditional "he" on a number of occasions and have also written of God, from time to time, as "our heavenly Parent." It should be understood by the reader that when the more traditional language is used, this does not imply that God is masculine; of course he is not! On the other hand, it would be misleading to say, as some do nowadays, that God is "beyond" or "above" sex. My contention would be that everything intended by our ordinary use of masculine and feminine terms should be applied, analogically, to God—he is not an "asexual" reality but is inclusive of all that human sexuality suggests, but without the limitations of our human sexual experience and understanding.

In a considerable number of books I have sought to interpret the essential affirmations of Christian faith through the use of the philosophical conceptuality nowadays styled Process Thought—a conceptuality which has its "founding father" in the Anglo-American thinker Alfred North Whitehead and which has had many representatives in North America and increasingly in other parts of the world. In my book *Process Thought and Christian Faith* (London: Nisbet, 1968; New York: Macmillan, 1968), I attempted to state succinctly the presuppositions of this conceptuality and the way in which it might be used in Christian theology. In the present book I shall not pursue this topic, but in the constructive chapters at the end I shall briefly summarize it and then seek to show how it may illuminate our understanding of the triunity of God.

I realize that some of my fellow "process thinkers" may disagree with the fashion in which I have argued. They would feel—indeed, some of them have said (e.g., Dr. John Cobb in a review of my book *The Holy Spirit* [Philadelphia: United Church Press, 1975] which appeared in the American journal *Religious Education* for May-June 1975)—that the kind of "distinction" which I propose between Word or Son and Spirit "makes little sense in the Whiteheadian conceptuality which [I] employ." In this book I try to profit from my friend's criticism, but I remain convinced that the prior allegiance of an exponent of Christian faith is to the theological tradition he or she inherits and by which he or she lives or tries to live. Hence I must seek to find some appropriate way, in the conceptuality of Process Thought, in which the central affirmation of that tradition can be maintained. I cannot say how successful I have been in this respect. But at least I can claim that my attempt has been twofold: first, to retain the great assertions of the inherited Christian faith; and second, to use a conceptuality which appears to me to be sound and true in an effort to make those assertions meaningful in our own day.

In conclusion, I would not wish it to be thought that I make any pretensions to finality or that I suppose that this relatively small book will settle all our problems. The best that I can say is that I have sought to be faithful to what I take to be the abiding convictions of the age-old Christian way of seeing God, the world, and humankind, while at the same time I have used a philosophical perspective which to me appears to be true, so far as we can know "the truth," and eminently useful for us today in the never-ending task of thinking through, once again, the significance of Christian faith. Perhaps others will be stimulated to carry on this task in a fashion more adequate than my own. I hope so.

Norman Pittenger
King's College
University of Cambridge

1
The
Palestinian
Experience

Many years ago Dr. C. C. J. Webb, the then Nolloth Professor of Philosophy of Religion at Oxford, used to tell the story of a Japanese savant who was visiting Britain and had attended a number of religious services in college chapels. The Japanese visitor had listened to the lessons read from the Bible during these services and had also noted the words of the prayers and hymns which were said or sung. According to Professor Webb, one day he made this remark: "I think I understand honorable Father, and I think I understand honorable Son. But I do not understand honorable pigeon."

This silly tale makes several points that are worth attention. First, that much Christian worship implies or states that the Christian conception of God includes a triunitarian aspect—a word which I prefer to "trinitarian," for reasons that will appear. Second, that the imagery frequently used in such worship is drawn from scriptural material which speaks of God as Father, of God as somehow present in or understood as Son, and of God portrayed as the Spirit—and for the last of these the picture of the dove, found both in the Old Testament and the New Testament, is often present. And third, that the whole conception cannot readily be understood, nor does it make much sense, unless there is somehow in the thought and experience of those who use it as well as those who hear it used some awareness of the specifically Christian mode of religious life. This third point is not the whole truth, to my mind, as I shall have occasion to argue; yet at the same time it is apparent that only those who do share something of this specific Christian life can grasp fully what triunitarian talk is all about.

Of course there are many who would deny that there is any lasting significance in such triunitarian talk about deity. Not only the groups calling themselves Unitarian, who descend mainly from earlier theologians who rightly discerned that the doctrine of the Trinity is not explicitly asserted in scripture, but also others who are engaged in the attempt to reconceive the inherited Christian faith, are inclined to think that this doctrine has little value today, save perhaps in a highly symbolic sense, and that it constitutes a serious obstacle to a meaningful rethinking of the Christian position as a whole.

What is more, there are many people who assume that the doctrine is an exercise in "celestial mathematics," with three somehow equaling one, and one somehow equaling three. Professor Webb himself, in his Oxford lectures on the subject, often said just this; but he went on to claim that the proper understanding of the doctrine is not along such lines at all, but rather has to do with an insight into the mystery of Godhead. To approach the doctrine as providing that insight and to seek to work out a way of formulating the significance of what is thus intimated can be, and for those who used to hear Dr. Webb's lectures most certainly was, a liberation from the fear that talk about "the holy and undivided Trinity" (to use a traditional expression) is nothing but absurd and nonsensical.

It is my own conviction that Webb's insistence on this way of approaching the ancient doctrine is right and will help us greatly in coming to terms with what at first sight appears to be meaningless or (at the very least) superfluous. Certainly for many today the traditional teaching about God as triune seems absurd. And it *is* absurd if we assume it to be about "celestial mathematics" or if we presumptuously claim that it provides a neat and completely plain "description" of what God is. But if it provides the insight to which Webb referred, if it is indeed an attempt to express conceptually, but by no means completely and neatly, the deepest meaning of Christian experience, it may have much to say to us. Furthermore, if it also makes possible a more profound understanding of God's ways with his world and with humankind, it may very well turn out to be a summary statement of "the Catholic faith"—which, in words from the *Quicunque Vult,* miscalled "the Athanasian Creed" (found in the 1662 Book of Common Prayer on page 67 and following), is this: "that we worship one God in Trinity, and Trinity in Unity."

For the triunitarian doctrine of God is not the creation of speculative theologians, although they have had their part in its formulation. It is based primarily on the living experience of men and women who believed that they were responding to God's activity in the world. They were familiar with the Jewish faith that through nature and history the one God of the universe is actively at work. They knew also that in Jesus Christ they had been in touch with a particular and decisive activity of God. And in their response to that activity, first in Jesus Christ and then more generally to that which "God is up to" in the whole world, they knew a reality greater than themselves which impelled them to such a new life of loving concern that it must (they were convinced) be more than their own human doing.

The threefold quality of this experience is behind the doctrinal formulations. These early Christians most certainly were monotheists, believing firmly in *one* God. How could the experience of "being in Christ" and of "sharing in the Spirit" be reconciled with this divine unity? Certain ancient distinctions, which they believed could be found in the Jewish scriptures and which were also to be discovered in the Gospels and other material in the New Testament, between God and his "Word" and his "Spirit," came to their help. Through long years of thought and study, always with reference to the continuing Christian life with God, the doctrine of the Triunity—of God as triune—finally emerged.

But there was more than that. The triune pattern, it was found, helped to make sense of wider human experience. Awareness of a creative source of the world, awareness of the diverse ways in which that source was disclosed in many ranges of human existence, and awareness of the capacity to grasp, through a response which was more than ordinary human rationality, that active creative source, however dimly or vaguely: here was a *vestigium Trinitatis*, as Augustine said, in ordinary human life. Somehow the triunitarian pattern illuminated the ordinary life of men and women, in secular as well as religious ways, in religion more generally as well as in Christian faith specifically.

Yet we must ask, once again, whether all this can still make sense. I am convinced that it can do so, provided we understand the way in which the doctrine came to be worked out, provided that we make no proud claims to an exhaustive knowledge of the "inner working" of the divine nature but are content to speak, again with Professor Webb, of "intimations and hints," and provided that we can employ a conceptuality, a wider pattern of thought, which will give a proper context or setting for what the doctrine is attempting to state. To argue this case is the purpose of the present book. It does not profess to be exhaustive or even to be adequate; rather, it seeks to suggest an approach, to present possibilities for our thinking, and to stress in particular the living, worshipful, inescapably real and compelling element in the traditional teaching. Perhaps others may wish to pursue the subject in more detail; I hope so. But I remain sure that basic Christian allegiance cannot afford to jettison the inherited view that God is no merely singular monad but is richly complex, both in his own nature and in his manner of working in the world.

Admittedly, a good deal of traditional discussion of the Godhead as triune has been altogether too precise, as if we were daring (in Leslie Stephen's words) to talk about God "with more precision than an entomologist would claim in describing the spots on a beetle." Humility, the recognition that we are speaking of the great mystery of the divine reality, and above all the understanding that we are to worship God, not define him, are necessary for us all. At the same time, there is wisdom in Augustine's dictum that we do better to speak thus haltingly and humbly about God than to say nothing at all about so great a mystery—a mystery with whom we have to do and about whom we are bound to try to come to some kind of understanding.

I have spoken of early Christian experience and thought. It is appropriate, therefore, to begin our discussion by an examination of the primitive Christian awareness, since it is there, not in speculative inquiry, that the triunitarian view finds its historical origin. Later on, we can turn to further developments and, in conclusion, seek for a way in which we may state, for our own time, something of what this view has to offer us if we wish to preserve and continue the religious awareness which goes by the name Christian.

The understanding of primitive Christian awareness must be through a study of the material in the New Testament. For in the books which go to make up that part of our Bible, we have the only available evidence for the way in which the first Christian believers lived, the faith which had won them, their earliest attempts to speak about both their life and their faith—a collection of data which must be examined carefully and with as much imagination as we can manage. I wish to stress this last, the need for imagination, because it is so easy to use the Bible as if it were a document whose main concern is theological and as if it provided us with clear and precise definitions. In the past a good deal of Bible reading and study treated it in just that way. Thus theologians worked with the assumption that they were dealing with something like a theological textbook; their task, on that assumption, was to arrange the given material in some consistent and coherent pattern. Of course not everything would fit neatly into this pattern, and hence *some* recognition of the variety or diversity of the writings was necessary. But this was felt to be regrettable because it seemed to make arrival at a simple, straightforward account of primitive Christianity incredibly difficult. The approach taken by such theologians overlooked the plain fact that when we read the various parts of the New Testament (whether they are fairly early in date, like the Pauline epistles, or fairly late, like the Johannine literature, the Pastoral Epistles, and the like), we are brought into touch with men and women possessed by a "first fine careless rapture," straining words to affirm a deep and mysterious experience and to point toward the greater surrounding mystery in relationship with which they were living as they worshiped, served, and sought to follow the Lord to whom they were utterly committed in faith. Really to understand what they said and what was written by them, we need imagination (as I have said)—and by this I mean an "empathetic" identification, a profound sympathy, or in other words what might well be styled an effort to enter with appreciation and with openness of mind and spirit into documents that come from another age and speak in another idiom than the one to which we are accustomed. Otherwise we shall be wooden, literalistic, perhaps even "fundamentalist" in our study of the biblical evidence, such as it is.

One thing is perfectly clear. There was absolutely no tritheism among early Christian believers. Tritheism is the notion that there are three "gods," rather than one God only. There have been some theologians who have urged that the first Christians accepted the God of Israel, whom their forefathers in Judaism had worshiped, but they added to this a belief in God as the Son, identifying the Son with Jesus risen from the dead and present with them following his resurrection, plus a belief in God known in the Christian community as the empowering and engracing which was so much a part of their experience. There were, then, these theologians have said, three quite diverse experiences, if not actually three different "gods"; and the work of the Christian thinkers of the first few centuries was to find some way of establishing that the three experiences or the three experienced "gods" were really one and the same God, the only God. Those who take this view assert, therefore, that the task of Christian theology in the period following New Testament times—roughly after A.D. 125— was to bring together into unity a *prior* three distinct aspects of Christian life and thought.

I believe that the truth is exactly the opposite of this notion. The first Christians, and after them the first who engaged in the theological task, were convinced of the unity of God. Being faithful to the Jewish tradition which they inherited and which they took as a matter of course, their problem was to discover how it might be possible, somehow or other, to incorporate into that abiding unity the patent fact that for them the God of Israel was also the God who had sent, and who was "in," the Jesus whom they worshiped and served; and that the Holy Spirit—the new, engracing, and empowering reality they knew in their fellowship—was also, somehow or other, equally divine, and divine in the only sense they could conceivably accept: namely, that he too was incorporated in the abiding unity of the God of Israel. The word for this, Trinity, makes its first appearance as the Greek *trias* in about A.D. 180 and appears to have been used initially by Theophilus of Antioch. What is important here, however, is not what word happened to be thought appropriate but the experience which is reflected in the New Testament as a whole.

There is some suggestion of a triunitarian view of God in one of the first three Gospels: namely, Matthew 28:19, where we read of the command supposed to have been given by the risen Lord to his disciples, that they were to baptize "in the name of the Father and of the Son and of the Holy Spirit." But most New Testament scholars doubt that these words are in fact dominical; they are more likely to be a deliverance from Christian experience in the Christian fellowship. In any event, they can hardly be taken as a specific and explicit instance of later triunitarian theology. So also with other supposed instances, such as the Holy Spirit "descending" on Jesus at his baptism, with the affirmation spoken by the Father that Jesus is God's "well-beloved Son," or, again, the account of the Annunciation of the Mother of Jesus, in which we read that she was "overshadowed" by the Spirit and informed by the angel Gabriel that her predicted son was God's Son.

In John's Gospel there is much talk about the Father, the Son, and the Holy Spirit, not least in the so-called Table Discourse after the Lord's Supper with his disciples. In passages like John 14: 11, 16 and following, and verse 26, the mutual relationships between Father and Son, Son and Spirit, Father and Spirit, etc., are indicated. But once again, most scholars would doubt that these are veridical words of Jesus himself and would say that they are part of a long meditation, put into Jesus' mouth to be sure, about the meaning of Christian life in Christ as empowered by the Spirit and relating believers through Christ in the Spirit to the heavenly Parent.

In the epistles in the New Testament there are frequent references to Jesus as the Son of God, just as there are frequent references to the Holy Spirit sent from God. There are phrases, which certainly have a triunitarian ring, in both 2 Corinthians (13:14) and 1 Corinthians (12:4–6), as well as in Peter's first letter (1 Peter 1:2, for instance), but no contemporary biblical scholar would assert that these are in any explicit sense statements of developed triunitarianism.

The effort to get from the New Testament any such precise doctrinal statement seems bound to fail. But this does not entail the conclusion that there is *no* triunitarianism in the material. On the contrary, there is a plain assertion that for the earliest Christians there was indeed what I have styled a "threefold experience," although this was not worked out theologically; it was a matter of life with God, known in Christ, through the Spirit present in the Christian fellowship. Let us turn, then, to a more summary statement of what that experience was all about, for it is

22

exactly there, in my judgment, that we shall be able to discover why the doctrine developed and what was its significance for Christian believers as it was thus developed.

The first Christians were believers in the one God of Israel, as I have already urged. They were monotheists of the strictest sort, rejecting entirely the "gods many and lords many" of their pagan neighbors. But who was this one God of Israel?

It is obviously impossible here to give an adequate account of the fashion in which the Jewish understanding of God moved from primitive fear and worship of sheer power to the full-orbed conception of God as the *chesed* or loving-mercy taught by the greatest of the prophets. But we can trace some significant stages in this movement. In the period known to scholars as Primitive Jahwism, God was regarded as associated with, if not identical with, the release of force in the world of nature and in human affairs. Volcanic eruption, earthquake, catastrophe on the historical level—and indeed all manner of violent and coercive activity—were assumed to be his work, and God himself was almost a personification of these destructive forces. But such a savage conception was enormously modified when Moses and those who followed him began to see that the power which was released in nature and human events was not sheer power without moral character; for them it was "the power that makes for righteousness," to use Matthew Arnold's well-known phrase.

Jahweh—a Hebrew word which was personal to God's own self-revelation and therefore deemed to be sacred—had, they believed from the earliest times of which we have any reliable information, chosen the Jewish people as particularly his own. There might be other divine beings; probably at an early stage their existence was taken for granted; but their God, Jahweh, was supreme and he had deigned to choose them as his agents in human affairs. When they went to battle other peoples, he was with them; if they were faithful to him, he would be faithful to them—indeed, he was *always* faithful to his purpose for them, and it was they who failed in the "covenant" established between God and the Jewish people.

But he was a God who was not only righteous himself but who demanded righteousness from his people. They must conduct themselves in accordance with his will; then they would be blessed and would "inherit the land" which he had promised to them. What began as a variety of very primitive power worship moved on, through the stage styled "henotheism"—each people had its god, yet the God of the Hebrews was supreme and above such other deities—to the conception of one moral God, who expected moral conduct from his own chosen people and who, through those called to speak in his name, provided the "laws" or commandments in terms of which that conduct was to be governed.

With the prophetic movement, a further advance was made. Now the righteous God was understood to be characterized by loving-mercy and a profound care for his people. Indeed, he loved them, was concerned in their affairs, and identified himself with their fortunes. He remained the *holy* One, never to be approached without utter reverence and awe; he tolerated no rivals; he was omnipotent in that all power derived ultimately from him; he required obedience to his commandments and would punish those who chose to disregard his will. Nonetheless, his innermost being was essentially loving-mercy. The way in which this was interpreted varied: in Amos, God's righteousness extended to all nations and peoples, in Hosea he was like a father to his people and wanted from them mercy rather than a merely ritual response (Hosea 6:6), in Isaiah he was "the high and lofty one" who was also "with those of a humble spirit," and in such fictional writings as the book of Jonah he was said to be eager to "save" Gentiles as well as Jews.

The Jews were his chosen people, to be sure; but this election was not for their own aggrandizement and self-satisfaction, even if over and over again common Jewish thought took such to be the case. His choice of the Jews, their noblest spokesmen believed, was for the purpose of bringing to the entire world, at least to that part of it then known, a knowledge of himself and an opportunity to serve him in peace and happiness. Even more important, however, God was ready to welcome and receive any who turned to him and sought in him their refuge, strength, and salvation.

The God of Israel was a God who *acted*—he was no inert "substance" or "being," but the "living God" who did things, who revealed himself through what he did, and who could therefore be known in terms of his "mighty works." Jews were not given to metaphysical conceptions, after the fashion of the Greeks; they did not think in abstract ways but were interested in concrete events. They pictured God in an imaginative fashion with the use of models drawn from their own experience and their own observation of the world. God was transcendent, but they did not use that word; rather, they spoke of him as "the high and lofty one who inhabiteth eternity." God was immanent, but instead of using such a term they said that he "came" into the world, "dwelt" among his people, "was present" in that which took place.

I have just sketched, briefly but I hope not inaccurately, the sort of picture the early Christians, as well as Jesus himself, inherited and in which they found meaning for existence. Yet for these first disciples of Jesus there was something more—and that something was absolutely primary in their thinking, as it was in their living. The God who was both living and active, both righteous and loving, both universal and also concerned with particular events, had in a signal fashion "determined, dared, and done" (in Christopher Smart's telling phrase) something new. He had acted supremely and decisively in a particular event, the event which is named when we say Jesus of Nazareth. Here as never before and nowhere else he had taken the initiative in "sending" Jesus and through Jesus in "visiting and redeeming his people." Doubtless this was not clearly thought out in the days when that Jesus had taught and acted in Palestine in what we call "the days of his flesh." Perhaps there had been glimpses or intimations of something special during that period; certainly there was a sense of the attractive yet awe-inspiring quality in his words and deeds. But Jesus was still a man, a fellow Jew whom they knew and followed and yet also revered and in one meaning of the word "feared"—he did not frighten or "scare" them, but in his presence they were aware of a more-than-human impact which made tremendous demands even as it won tremendous devotion.

What Jesus thought about himself we do not know. Certainly, despite occasional language in the Fourth Gospel, he did not think of himself as divine. He may not even have regarded himself as the Messiah or agent of God who according to Jewish expectation would one day "bring in the kingdom of God" in the world. Probably he felt that he was in the prophetic tradition, but with a different mission and message from the expected one. For in his teaching he represented God as not only welcoming and accepting Love but more significantly as seeking, initiating, or, to use a theological term, "prevenient" Love. God went out to seek and find those who were lost, those who needed assistance, those who wanted loving. Jesus not only taught this; he acted it out in his own conduct, for he delighted in the company of outcasts, "the lost sheep of the house of Israel," the unwanted, the unloving, the rejected and condemned.

Finally he was crucified, obedient to what he took to be God's intention for him. Very likely he came to the conviction that only in this way, through obedience to the point of death, could he disclose and impart the reality which evidently possessed him completely: the reality of God as loving Parent, we might even say as cosmic Lover, whose care for his people would go to any lengths and would accept suffering, anguish, even death, if this would bring to his children a full and abundant life, *shalom* or harmonious and truly human existence in and under his loving yet demanding care.

And there came also the cluster of experiences which we call the resurrection. This Jesus had been killed; he had died. Yet he had not been annihilated by this death, for "he could not be holden of it"—he was still with his disciples, in renewed power and with even more intimate identification of himself with them. He had been "raised from among the dead" and "death had no more dominion over him." In John Masefield's words in *The Trial of Jesus*, "he had been let loose into the world, where neither Jew nor Roman could stop him."

The God of Israel had acted, supremely and decisively, in the total fact of Jesus, living among men, crucified, dead, risen again, still a presence and a power in the world. There was something further; this was a quickening of life for those who responded to this Jesus, so strong yet so persuasive, so personal yet so much a matter of the Christian fellowship's very existence, so much more than seemed possible in strictly human terms, that it could only be taken as still another activity of God himself, the God of Israel who had sent his Son into the world as and in Jesus. The Spirit was now released in a new way as men and women responded in faith, obedience, worship, and service to this Jesus. This was *divine* Spirit and not just an intensive and special working of the human heart and mind.

Notice that this is not a series of events: first the God of Israel, then the appearance of Jesus, and finally the "fellowship of the Holy Spirit." As Karl Barth has correctly insisted, the truth of the matter is that from the very first, once the victory of Jesus over death had been accomplished, there was a complex yet unitary reality. In the risen Lord the God of Israel was particularly at work ("uniquely," if we wish to use the word), and this working was known and accepted in faith through the Spirit whose activity was precisely to establish the truth about the risen Lord.

What Jesus had taught and done, in his days in Palestine, he was recognized as having himself embodied or "en-manned" or enacted; the very Love which is God himself, coming to seek and save, was expressed visibly in this human life and its consequences. Had Jesus only taught, he would have been a great sage or prophet and no more; had he only acted, he would have been a noble and splendidly compelling example. Because he *was* in himself, as the insight of faith now realized, just that which he taught and did, he was an act of the God who is Love, *the* act which provided the clue or key to all of God's working in the world and among men. "In Christ, God was reconciling the world unto himself." In him, "the Word"—or God's self-expressive activity—"was made flesh."

Here, then, we have a threefold experience answering to a threefold yet unitary fact. This is the primitive Christian reality, first in Palestine and then elsewhere in the Greco-Roman world of the time. There had been, maybe, intimations of such an act in the earlier days of Jewish history; perhaps the sages and prophets had foreseen that God would act in this way, since this was the way in which a God such as they believed to be supreme might well one day act. So at any rate the first Christians thought; therefore they "searched the scriptures"—the Jewish sacred writings—to find if there were such intimations and hints and expectations. In doing this, they may have twisted texts out of their natural meaning and read into them more than was originally there. Nevertheless, their instinct was right, because they were convinced through their Jewish heritage that a purpose ran through all history, that God was active in that history, and that he was able to vindicate himself by fresh acts which would plainly disclose what was the intention he had for his creation.

The overall impression which one gets as one reads the books of the New Testament with imagination and sympathetic feeling is very plain indeed. Here was a new community of men and women who were filled with vitality, characterized by deep faith, living in love and in hope—despite the obvious fact that they were at the same time, like all the rest of us, often self-seeking, narrow-minded, quarrelsome, frequently hard to get along with, by no means perfect human beings. The language they used to speak about their experience and about the facts upon which that experience was based is often confused and contradictory. There is no nice, neat, precise, and exact system of doctrine; we are greatly mistaken if we look for any such thing. But there is something greater: a fellowship of human beings grasped by a faith which they cannot escape, empowered by a spirit (a Spirit, rather) which holds them together, and a "joy and peace in believing," coupled with a quality of moral life, which attracted many and won converts wherever Christians happened to go.

This needed somehow to be formulated or worked out in a consistent and coherent manner. It was the task of the Patristic Age, during the first four centuries of the Christian enterprise, to do just this. In the next chapter we shall follow this development and see what emerged; that is, we shall study the development of the doctrine of the Triunity of God, which we ourselves have inherited and of which we are obliged to make sense, in our own time, with our own outlook, and in language which will be meaningful to us. In this necessary task, however, we can never forget those words from the *Quicunque Vult*: "the Catholic Faith is this: that we *worship* one God in Trinity and Trinity in Unity."

For Further Reading

It may be helpful in understanding the chapter just concluded if some nontechnical books are listed which will enable the reader to follow more fully the line of argument which I have presented, more particularly in respect to the interpretation of New Testament material.

In my judgment the most satisfactory treatment is to be found in three small books by Prof. John Knox, formerly of Union Theological Seminary in New York: *The Man Christ Jesus, Christ the Lord,* and *On the Meaning of Christ.* These three books, together with Dr. Dennis Nineham's Pelican commentary on *St. Mark* and the other volumes in that Pelican series, provide an excellent background for and also a summary statement of the position which I take to be sound. Although there is considerable difference in minor matters of detail and, as between Professors Knox and Nineham, on the one hand, and the other contributors to the Pelican series, on the other, in the way of presenting the relationship of the "historical Jesus" to the Christ of the Christian community's faith, all will be seen to adopt the same attitude toward the experience of the Christians in primitive days and their first tentative attempt to state the meaning of that experience.

Since I have devoted considerable space to the development of the Jewish understanding of God, I wish here to observe that I have no intention of rejecting the conviction that God was indeed active in self-revelation during that period. The Old Testament is a witness to the ways in which (and they were various and often almost contradictory from time to time) that activity of God was understood and expressed by men of deep insight and profound faith. If William Temple was correct in speaking of revelation as "the divinely guided coincidence of divine activity and inspired human response," the Old Testament is a classic instance of just such a situation. The reader may find the relevant articles (on the various books of the Old Testament and on the history of Jewish thought) in the *Interpreter's Bible* and also in R. H. Pfeiffer's *Introduction to the Old Testament*, helpful for a beginner in this kind of study. In any good commentary (e.g., Black's series, Moffatt's series, or the Cambridge University Press series), references will be found to the more advanced and scholarly work which has been going on for a hundred years. My concern in this note is only to offer assistance to the ordinary reader who has neither time for nor interest in this specialist area, but does wish to have a general view of the work done in both Old and New Testament by reverent, honest, and well-informed scholars.

2
The
Patristic
Formulation

The formal statement of the doctrine of God's triunity was worked out over several centuries, beginning with the fact of Christian experience (as the last chapter sought to demonstrate) and moving toward a theological position whose purpose was to preserve the reality of that fact but also to state it in a coherent fashion. The development was no enterprise of idle speculation but a necessary movement of thought for those who believed that the threefold meeting with God as "over us, God with us, and God in us," in H. E. W. Turner's admirable phrasing *(Dictionary of Christian Theology* [London: SCM Press, 1969], p. 345), was neither accidental nor incidental but absolutely basic and essential.

Inevitably this work had to be done with the use of the conceptual tools that were then available. Frequently enough, contemporary writers fault the fathers of the church for their use of such tools. Such critics seem to suppose that it might have been possible to do the job which was required in the church, but to do it without any reference to or reliance upon the prevailing patterns of thought. The truth of the matter is that none of us, however much we may try, can think through a problem without employing the philosophical ideas that are present in our time and place. Even those who claim that they are entirely without such ideas are inevitably, if unconsciously, presupposing some such notions.

For instance, is it possible to work out a "biblical theology" which is entirely independent of any so-called "secular" thought? Surely it has become clear enough, after the fact, that even the most "independent" efforts have in one way or another been influenced by nonbiblical concepts. In recent years Karl Barth and Emil Brunner have sought to work out a strictly "biblical theology." Yet we can now see, once we look at the results of their labors, that, far from this presumed "independence," they are dependent upon ideas that were derived from sources that are not, strictly speaking, biblical. Brunner was in violent reaction to the liberal idealism of much continental and especially German philosophy, but he thought and wrote in post-Kantian terms and was profoundly influenced by the existentialism of Kierkegaard and others—as he himself practically admitted in his later writings. Karl Barth was equally antagonistic to philosophical theology in its traditional form, attacking such procedures as the use of analogy of being and the like; but he also was plainly post-Kantian in his position, was influenced by existentialist views (explicitly in his earliest work and, despite his disavowal of such influence, also in later books), and throughout his life could not escape from the nineteenth century's sharp distinction between the deliverances of "pure reason" (scientific or logical) and those of the deepest kind of "practical reason," insofar as this meant that there is a kind of awareness or knowledge which is derived from and appeals to the nonscientific and nonlogical aspect or element in human experience. All his talk about nothing but revelation, even his insistence that the very receiving of revelation is God's activity with no human capacity involved, can be seen to reflect precisely the dichotomy which Kant established and which thinkers after Kant developed. Both these great theologians, furthermore, were in the line that descends from René Descartes, with his sharp distinction between *res extensa* and *res cogitans,* the realms of matter and of mind—and it is due to this influence, rather than to any specifically biblical material, that both tended to say very little about the world of nature, of sticks and stones and things material, putting all their emphasis on history and to some degree on human experience. Both were led to the absurd position, which through them became an almost universally accepted theological position, that history and nature are not (as common sense shows they most certainly *are*) intimately related. History has a geography, so to say; this is an inescapable fact which they overlooked or forgot.

Now all this means that the way in which we read biblical material is bound to be determined by the presuppositions which consciously or unconsciously we bring to the reading. The virtue of the fathers of the church, in their working out of a formal doctrine of God and of God's relationship with his world, is their awareness of the nonbiblical outlook, quite as much as their intention to be true, so far as was possible, to the biblical data. The way in which they proceeded depended upon their conviction that God was known not only through the story which the Bible tells about him and his activity but also through the philosophers, sages, and other thinkers of nonbiblical provenance. With the exception of a few, like Tertullian, they were hospitable toward such deliverances of wise men and profound thinkers. And to my mind this is all to their credit. The particular philosophy or philosophies which these fathers took for granted may not appeal to us; indeed, I for one am convinced that neither middle- nor neo-Platonism are helpful and that their use led the early theologians to say many things that are radically different from the basic faith of which the scriptures are a witness. At the same time, as we read them we know where we are, and we can appreciate that with such concepts as were available to them they did the best they could do— the best that could be done, to be frank, under those circumstances, with those presuppositions, and always with the intention of giving meaning to and finding a meaning in the abiding reality of the experience of Christian men and women in their time.

I do not apologize for this long excursus, since it is only with some such awareness of the actual patristic situation that we can come to an appreciative understanding of their accomplishment. But let us turn to the actual development of thought about God as triune, as these devoted believers who were also intellectually acute men worked at the problem: how somehow to incorporate into a fundamental monotheistic faith in God the threefold experience of fact and the threefold facts of experience. In sketching this development I am indebted to two admirable articles by Prof. Christopher Stead of Cambridge, published in *Theology* in October and November 1974 under the title "The Origins of the Doctrine of the Trinity," as well as to such established histories as those by the late Dr. J. F. Bethune-Baker (*History of Early Christian Doctrine* [London: Methuen], first published in the early part of the century, ninth edition in 1951), whose work remains classic, even if it requires correction in matters of detail; and also to J. N. D. Kelly's *Early Christian Doctrines* (London: Black, 1958). In each of these volumes a full bibliography is provided. For the general reader I may also mention Turner's excellent summary article in *Dictionary of Christian Theology*, mentioned at the start of this chapter.

In all these books, and in many others as well, another important point is continually stressed—and rightly so. Although the Fathers entertained the presuppositions of the culture of their own age and naturally assumed the philosophical outlook which was prevalent at the time, they were concerned to emphasize the continuity of the Christian event with what had gone before it in Jewish history. Their way of doing this was by using the Jewish sacred writings as providing what we might call source material for their construction of a doctrinal statement. They saw there adumbrations of the threefoldness to which we have regularly referred, adumbrations which were to their mind plain enough in the Jewish scriptures. The frequency with which those scriptures refer to the Word of God, the Wisdom of God, and the Spirit of God appeared to them to indicate a Jewish awareness of a certain kind of plurality in the divine ways of working in the world. Certainly it was always the one God who was at work; but the attribution of this or that act, this or that event, this or that response, to Word or Wisdom or Spirit did not appear purely accidental to the Fathers. Rather, that attribution pointed toward distinctions which were significant and, for Christian theological purposes, both suggestive and helpful. We shall see how they were able thus to establish a correspondence between this Jewish terminology and their own more philosophical notions.

We should be clear that with this intention of working out, on the basis of the Jewish scriptures and the religious faith to which they bore witness, the meaning of the new experience of God in Christ and the presence and power of the Spirit in the fellowship of the faithful, the fathers of the church were in no conscious sense engaged in a distortion of the tradition which they had received from the very earliest days. We should be in grave error if we assumed that these devout and thoughtful men would willingly have modified that tradition. Our point is quite different. We are making only two comments. The first is that all of us, in every culture and at every time, must necessarily work with the presuppositions and assumptions that are part of the air we breathe. Usually we are not conscious of the degree to which these influence our thought, but that we are thus influenced is a plain fact. The second comment is that in the Patristic Age these presuppositions and assumptions made the Fathers see things in a particular way and employ categories which have their particular meaning in that particular age. The result can very well be a shift in emphasis or a change in interpretation—just as one pair of spectacles may give a different picture from the one that would be given if another pair of spectacles were worn or if one attempted to look at things without the aid of any spectacles at all. As a matter of fact, the last of these is impossible for men; inevitably we see things through this or that accepted pair of eyeglasses, worn simply because those are the only ones available to us at the moment. Without spectacles we do not see at all.

A simple example here is the common acceptance in the Patristic Age of the concept of substance (*ousia*, in Greek) as the basic reality in all that is known and experienced. We today are much more likely to accept the concept of activity, energy, happening, or event as the fundamental reality in the world. Centuries of thought, including in recent years the newer physics which talks about *quanta* rather than about fixed and determinate entities which (so to say) bump up against one another and are arranged in an equally fixed and determinate fashion, have so familiarized us with temporal change, with the experience and observation of the world as anything but fixed and determinate, and with a continuing stress on the dimension of space-time rather than on Newtonian concepts of space in which persistent substances have attached to them primary or secondary "qualities"—all this has made the concept of such substance alien to our mode of interpretation and understanding. In place of these we are more likely to emphasize the flow of experience and the primacy of event. But for the Patristic Age this was not the case; in that age Platonic and Aristotelian notions of substance were taken for granted. Thus the fathers naturally used this category, among others, in their reading of scripture and in their development of the theological implications of the witness borne by scripture. They did not see—indeed, they could not see—how the category of "substance," applied to God, man, and the world, would result in damage to the Christian experience of the living God, active in the world, responding to the world, and loving his creatures.

When the then prevalent notion that perfection equaled absolute unchangeability or immutability was also accepted, again unconsciously but simply because this was taken for granted thanks to Hellenistic presuppositions, even more tragic consequences could and did result. There is no way in which the reality of the divine activity as both effecting events in the world and being affected by those events in the world can be reconciled with the conviction that God, as perfect, is entirely unchangeable and immutable. The Fathers wrestled mightily with this problem; to some degree their way of stating the triunitarian doctrine of God is a reflection of their difficulty, because somehow or other they were obliged to bring together the Hebrew-Christian *given*—God in unceasing contact with and always aware of (as well as responding to) a world where change and movement take place—with a presupposed belief that to talk about God is to talk about the absolutely changeless. It did not occur to them, nor should we expect that it might have occurred to them, that perfection might mean not absolute changelessness but faithfulness in purpose which was yet open to infinite adaptation, affected by the creation but not deflected from that purpose. Even today many seem to find this an incredibly difficult if not impossible view; they interpret the familiar words of the Compline collect which speak of God's "eternal changelessness" as a metaphysical statement about God's sheer immutability, instead of grasping that the collect can just as well (and more biblically) be interpreted as referring to the utter faithfulness of God in his loving care and concern for the world and in that sense, only in that sense, meaningfully spoken of as "unchangeable."

We are now in a position to sketch the patristic development of the doctrine of God's triunity. There were two possible lines of thought: one was to speak of the threefoldness as in some sense a matter of modes of the one divine life and activity; the other was to speak of it as involving some sort of grading, by which full deity could be attributed to the Father, a lesser sort of deity to the Word, and still less complete divine reality to the Spirit. And in each of these possible lines of thought there were several different ways open for adoption. The one thing that was not possible for the Patristic Age was tritheism, in which Father, Word, and Spirit could be seen as each of them "God" but brought into unity only in a fashion which would have minimized the unity in order to stress the threeness. Such an approach would have been unthinkable to them. For it to have been possible would have demanded the introduction of a *fourth* "something," a divine quality which was distinct from, yet in some fashion found within, each of the three called Father,

Word, and Spirit. This would have been pluralism with a vengeance. Even when, with the Cappadocian Fathers (Basil of Caesarea, Gregory of Nazanzius, and Gregory of Nyssa, whose work was carried on in the fourth century), the analogy of "three men," Peter, James, and John, was suggested, any notion of pluralism of a tritheist sort cannot be sustained; and this for the simple reason that all three were Hellenistic thinkers and biblically oriented as well. Their biblical awareness made anything like a denial or questioning of monotheism impossible, while their Hellenizing background made it equally impossible to think of "three men," like Peter, James, and John, as if they were not one through their very shared manhood, a manhood that existed, so to say, *in* and not distinct from each of them.

The first type of "mode" triunity to be developed is found in Asia Minor and elsewhere in the second century. At least some thinkers (e.g., Noetus) were prepared to say that the Father, the Son, and, later, the Spirit were modes in which the one God manifested himself; these modes were successive in character, so that "when the Father deigns to be born and to suffer, he is the Son," as Noetus himself is reported to have said. In a more developed form, this type of modalism was taught by Sabellius in the early third century. Sabellius seems to have believed that while God is indeed an absolute unity, he reveals himself in the world as Father, then as Son (or Word), and finally as Spirit; each was divine, but they were not simultaneously operative—rather, as with earlier modalism, one followed upon the other.

On the other hand, there was also a kind of modalism which could speak in terms of the various simultaneous "dispensations" or "economies": creation, redemption, and inspiration, proper to Father, Word, and Spirit respectively. Some reflection of this approach may be found in a number of thinkers like Theophilus of Antioch, Irenaeus, and even in the later thinker Tertullian. While the *language* of modalism, strictly speaking, was not used by them, the idea of modalism—or differing "modes of revelation"—most certainly was present. Here there was not talk of a successive series of divine manifestations but of abiding or permanent ways in which God was disclosed and known.

This kind of triunity had one defect, to which succeeding Christian thinkers called attention. By speaking either of successive manifestations or of merely "economic" disclosure—that is, only in the functioning of God in the world but not in the very being of the Godhead—modalism of this sort appeared to make a sharp distinction between the reality of God in himself and the ways in which God acted in his creation. But if the way in which God acted in creation was *genuinely* revelatory of that which God was in himself, it was pointed out, then there must of necessity be some correspondence between Father, Word or Son, and Spirit known in the creation and the very reality of God himself. To put this in formal terms, the Triunity is not only "economic," not only a matter of divine functioning or activity. It is also "essential" to the divine existence as such; it must have some ontological grounding.

In the Eastern Church, the work of Origen is crucial. This great theologian, who lived from about A.D. 185, to the middle of the third century and whose work was done largely in Alexandria, taught that the Word of God who in Jesus had been incarnate was "eternally generated" by the Father; so also the Spirit was to be seen as "produced" by the Father, although talk about the Spirit was by him confined largely to the life of the Christian community and the Christian believer. Origen would not have approved the use made of his teaching by the heretic Arius, who in the early years of the fourth century interpreted the "eternal generation" of the Son to mean that the latter was so subordinate to the Father that he could not be regarded as divine in the fullest sense but was a "creature" (although not a creature like other created beings, but of a higher kind). The Spirit was also a "creature," and in his case the level of his "created divinity," as we might style it, was even less than the Son's. Origen had spoken, to be sure, of a "subordination" of the Son to the Father, but it is evident that his intention was not to make this suggest the Son's "creaturehood," only to maintain the Father's priority in godhead. Arius had a different intention: in his famous saying, "There was a time when the Son was not," the subordination was so presented as to deny the full reality of God incarnate in Jesus, while from the point of view of the doctrine of Jesus Christ he was unable to assert, with the main Christian tradition, a truly redeeming and saving God in one who entirely shared the human lot.

Arius was condemned at the first Council of Nicaea in A.D. 325. His opponent was Athanasius, at that time a deacon of the church in Alexandria but in later years bishop and world-famous theological exponent of the *homoousios,* teaching that the Word or Son in Jesus is "of one substance with the Father" and hence "able to save to the uttermost" as only true God can save.

The Cappadocians, to whom reference has already been made, were greatly influenced by Origen, but they took a line very different from that of Arius. At the same time they insisted that the Spirit must also be fully divine. Professor Turner has stated their position succinctly in his essay in the *Dictionary of Christian Theology* (p. 347): "Using the logical distinction between universals and particulars, they defined the universal of the Trinity as uncreatedness and Godhead and the modes of being or differentiating particulars of the three particulars as ingeneracy [the Father], generation [the Son], and procession [the Spirit] respectively." In respect to the Spirit, they sought to demonstrate both from the scriptural portrayal of the work of the Spirit in inspiring and giving life and from the worship and devotion of succeeding Christian experience, that just as the Word or Son must be "of one substance with the Father" and hence fully divine, so also must the Spirit be *homoousios.* Thus within the unity of God there are three "particulars" or differentiations, each of which is fully divine and all of which are mutually indwelling.

The greatest contribution of the Cappadocians, however, was in their recognition that the language used about God needed to be as precise and exact in reference as possible, so that ambiguities would be avoided. The word *ousia* applied to the unity of Godhead; the word *hupostasis* was to be employed for each of the "differentiations." *Ousia* is commonly translated as "substance" or "essence," since in Latin *substantia* or *essentia* are its usual equivalents. *Hupostasis* has been translated as "person," following here the usage of Tertullian, who in the previous century (his dates are approximately A.D. 160 to 220) had written about God as "one substance, three persons." Unhappily the contemporary meaning of "person," as we are inclined to use it, is by no means identical with the sense intended by the Cappadocians or by Tertullian himself. For us it suggests a subjective center of experience, a psychological selfhood. But for the Patristic Age *persona* meant either what we would call a mask, such as was worn by actors on the stage in the Greco-Roman world—hence we speak today of the cast of a play as *dramatis personae*—or a legal entity under Roman law. The original Greek word *hupostasis*, however, had a different meaning from the Latin sense of *persona*. Its basic theological significance was defined by the Cappadocians as an objective, concrete, and enduring reality. It is in that sense, then, that the Father, Word, and Spirit may be called hypostases.

The word *ousia* can also have two meanings in Hellenistic thought. It can mean the basic underlying reality which any given thing *is*; it can also mean the particular reality of that given thing. Thus it might point to the simple fact of Godhead as the deepest truth about Father, Son, and Spirit; and this was its use by the Cappadocians, as we have seen, where the *ousia* is the divine "uncreatedness." Before them, however, its second meaning was often approximately identical with that of *hupostasis*; hence the frequent confusion in terminology in pre-Cappadocian discussion of the divine triunity. After them, however, and thanks to their terminological precision, *hupostasis* was restricted to the differentiations (Father, Word or Son, and Spirit), while *ousia* was employed only for the "god-ness" of deity.

We cannot pursue this history in any further detail, but we must say a few words about Augustine, who in the early years of the fifth century (he lived from A.D. 354 to 430) developed for the Western Church a doctrine of God as triune which is characterized by great subtlety, psychological insight, and the effort to be loyal to the witness both of the scriptures and the Christian tradition. In his *De Trinitate*, which along with the *Confessions* and *The City of God* represents Augustine at his noblest and most persuasive, he accepted the divine unity in substance, in majesty, in activity, and in will. He stressed this unity to the point of insisting that even in that which God "does in the creation," the unity is present: *opera Trinitatis ad extra sunt indivisa*—the works of God externally (in creation, revelation, redemption, and inspiration) are absolutely indivisible. Hence in each of these "works," the whole Godhead is involved and active. On the other hand, the several works are "appropriated" to the differentiations of Father (creation), Son (revelation and redemption), and Spirit (inspiration). If this be the case, all attempts to talk about the differentiations as "persons" in the modern sense are excluded. Rather, Augustine offers us two analogies. One is the psychological, in which memory, will, and understanding may be differentiated but yet each of these is nothing other than *una mens* (one mind). The other analogy is drawn from the experience of love, in which the lover, the loved one, and the loving relationship between the first two are a unity which also include distinctions.

Augustine employs the latter analogy on one occasion; most frequently he prefers the psychological analogy. But in each case he is talking of *relations*. These relations, between Father and Son and Spirit, are essential to God; they are eternal in him but are manifested in his ways of working in the world. They are reciprocal in him; and in his creative, revelatory (and redeeming), and inspiring activity they are revealed and mutually involved, each one with the other two. This Augustinian teaching that the distinctions are relations was taken over by Thomas Aquinas, the greatest of the scholastic theologians of the Middle Ages. At the same time, Aquinas accepted the definition of *persona* given by Boethius in the sixth century (*persona* for Boethius signified "an individual substance of a rational nature"); and his attempt to bring this definition into accord with Augustine's stress on relation presents serious problems. Can we have it both ways or must we settle for one or the other?

Thomas Aquinas' formulation of the doctrine of God as triune became the normative statement for Western Christendom in succeeding centuries. Unfortunately, in popular devotion his insistence (and that of his predecessors) upon the divine unity has not always been grasped; far too many "simple Christians" talk and think of "trinity in unity" as meaning that somehow there are three "gods" who are yet "one" in an undefined sense. "God the Father, God the Son, and God the Holy Spirit" certainly suggests to many that there are "three" who are all of them divine, whereas a phrasing like "God who is Father, Son, and Holy Spirit" would be both more precise and less likely to lead to a species of tritheism. The mistake is made more serious by the use of the English word "person" in so many hymns and devotional exercises, leading those who hear or say it to assume that the word is to be taken in its modern sense.

Sometimes in the writing of our own contemporaries the error is compounded. Thus we have had talk about "three centers of consciousness," as if God were a society composed of three psychological selves. Furthermore, the simple identification of "Word" with "Son" has suggested for many that God in his second distinction or relation (the Word) is exhaustively present in and active through the man Jesus; this has led some to explain the Triunity of God by speaking of God the Father, his Son Jesus, and the Spirit. This is christological error, since it fails to make the necessary distinction between Jesus' manhood and God incarnate in that manhood. What is more, it erroneously implies that in his revelatory and redemptive activity God works exclusively in and through Jesus. Hence those who have not heard of Jesus or (having heard of him) do not believe in him are presumed to have no possibility of knowing anything about God save by the exercise of their human reason toward some First Cause or Supreme Being. And, beyond that, they have no hope of finding "salvation" because they are not in touch with this single instance of God's redemptive work in the world. In each case this is a contradiction of the early church's position. Christologically, the Fathers recognized God's working apart from the specific instance of Jesus. Soteriologically, or in respect to human redemption, those same Fathers sought to emphasize the centrality and decisive quality of God's work in Jesus while at the same time they were ready to welcome any and every manifestation of goodness, truth, righteousness, beauty, and love as both disclosing something of God to his children and also, when faithfully followed, providing opportunity for fellowship with God sufficient to open the way to a "saved life." In the mainstream of Christianity, both East and West, it has never been said that those without knowledge of Jesus Christ are to be regarded as eternally damned—although we must admit that in some of the churches whose teaching reflects strictly post-Reformation theologizing such an attitude is by no means unknown.

I believe that we shall get much farther in our thinking if we use the term Word (equivalent to Logos in the New Testament, as in John's Gospel) for all that is done by God toward and with his creatures; the Word is not only essential in the very being of God, but whatever God does is "by the Word, through whom all things were made, who is the light that lighteneth every man." The term Son is more appropriately applied to the *incarnate* Word—that is, to Jesus himself, in whom "the Word was made flesh and dwelt among us, full of grace and truth." This careful distinction will save us from error and from uncharitable "imperialism" as Christian people. Admittedly the two terms,

Word and Son, were eventually used practically co-terminously in the Patristic Age. We may consider this to have been unfortunate and misleading, as it is, and yet we can usually tell, when reading these ancient writers, whether they were intending reference to the "eternal Word" *or* to the "incarnate Word," Jesus as Son of God.

The confusion to which I have just adverted is responsible for some of the modern mis-representations of triunitarian doctrine. An undergraduate in my own college was greatly puzzled by the words in the Series Two Communion Service of the Church of England, where it is said, immediately after a reference to Jesus Christ, that "through him" God has made the world. How, he asked, could God have made the world through a historic figure who appeared long after the world began? Efforts to show him that the traditional doctrine of *communicatio idio-matum* (which tells us that we may apply to the single "person of Jesus Christ" that which is said of his divine and human natures) made this usage possible, hardly succeeded in meeting his problem. He went on to inquire whether, in that case, Jesus was really a man at all; and why, if there is a distinction between what is said of Jesus as a man and whatever God is doing in and through him, this is not clearly stated. His problem was primarily christological, of course, but it was more than that. He was pointing, albeit uncon-sciously, to the confusion in triunitarian teaching which such terminology creates.

It remains to say something about some quite recent work done on the doctrine of God as triune. Two theologians may be selected: Leonard Hodgson, my own beloved teacher who for many years was Regius Professor of Theology in Oxford and who died a few years ago, and Karl Barth, the great Swiss theologian whose enormous *Church Dogmatics* has been more influential than any other theological work of our time. I believe that Barth's way of speaking of God's triunity is the better of the two and merits close attention; Hodgson's position, as expounded in his *The Doctrine of the Trinity* (London: Nisbet, 1943), is too dependent upon the social analogy for it to be taken as in the main line of triunitarian thought.

Hodgson's starting point is Christian religious experience. That experience, he believes, is responsive to God's revelation of himself to his children. In revelation God has disclosed himself as creator, as redeemer, and as inspirer: as the Father, the Son (Hodgson does not distinguish as carefully as I have urged between Son and Word), and the Spirit. Each of these disclosures gives a meeting with God, and Christian experience is living in terms of those meetings. Hence we start with a basic threeness and must find some way of arriving at a unity. The unity, however, is not a strictly mathematical oneness; it is qualitative, and its nature is better intimated in man in his social relationships. Here, then, is a social Trinity which Hodgson is prepared to follow through to the point of interpreting the "persons" in the Godhead as being centers of consciousness, each of them therefore a psychological self.

Hodgson singles out the love analogy of Augustine as useful for his purposes, but he does not balance this (despite his interesting use of psychological language) with Augustine's more unitary analogy of the self as *una mens* in memory, will, and understanding. Yet he does go on to say that the three met in Christian experience are also in a very real sense indicative of God's own nature; his theology is not merely functional or "economic" but attempts to be thoroughly ontological. God must have in himself a corresponding threeness, but this is thoroughly social in nature and not a matter of relations as in, say, Thomas Aquinas. With his desire to emphasize the priority of experience to theology, Hodgson is even prepared to say that Christian life is nothing less than a participation in the life of God himself—we are, so to say, taken "into" the Trinity.

Karl Barth takes an entirely different approach. For him, as the very first volume of the *Church Dogmatics* shows, the triunity of God is so much a matter of divine revelation that his entire theological system starts with it as given in God's act of self-disclosure. In the immediacy of

God's action in Jesus Christ we have the Father sending the Son whose coming is known only through the working of the Spirit. I believe that this insistence on the unity of the divine revelatory act is sound and true to the New Testament material; but the problem with Barth is his exclusive christocentrism, in which Jesus Christ is the one and only, the unique and unparalleled, act of God's coming to men. Here he is not as faithful to scripture as he would claim, for reasons already given in an earlier paragraph. On the other hand, Barth stresses that in God himself as the essential Godhead the basic reality is *God as active:* he is Love and his being is in his loving act, both in himself and outwardly in the creation.

Again Barth urges that the right meaning of the divine distinctions (the "persons") is to be found, not in our own contemporary sense of person, but in the concept of "modes of being"—here he follows the Cappadocian terminology and sees each *hupostasis* as concrete, objective, and eternal in God himself. To speak of the hypostases as *tropeis*, with those ancient Fathers, seems to Barth to be the most satisfactory procedure; and *tropeis* does in fact translate as "modes of being" and hence also (since God's being and his act are identical) as modes of activity.

I welcome Barth's stress on God as the active God, the living God, the loving God. Whatever may be erroneous in his excessive claim for Jesus Christ as the single act of God for revelation and redemption, he is surely correct in his rejection of anything approaching tritheism; he is entirely biblical in his teaching that God is himself present where he is at work; and the conclusion that what God is and what God does constitute a unitary reality, but with appropriate distinctions, is certainly sound. For God to be God, Barth says, is for him to be Father, Word, and Spirit; there is no other God, nor can there be if Christian revelation is taken with entire seriousness. In his later writings, notably in his little book *The Humanity of God*, Barth is prepared to go so far as to say that in his humanward movement God shows himself to be possessed of everything that humanity, once perfected and brought to the fullness of the divine intention, possesses or could possess. All this is in God himself. Thus he makes clear that "God is for man" (and, I should add, for the whole creation) precisely because in the richness of the divine unity God himself *is* what man in a creaturely fashion is *to become*. Not that God and man are identical in any ontological sense, of course, but rather because God is never the immutable and unaltered metaphysical perfection of Hellenistic thought but rather is the living God whose doing is one with his being. He does create, he does reveal and redeem, he does inspire; because he does these, what these essentially are is what God everlastingly is.

3
Experiential Awareness

At the end of the last chapter, I spoke favorably about Karl Barth's triunitarian theology, as contrasted with that of Leonard Hodgson. But I also indicated that I believed Hodgson to be correct in his conviction that what might be called triunitarian religion or religious experience is prior to, and the condition for, theological formulation. Hodgson is inclined to speak as if the experience of Father, Word or Son, and Holy Spirit had been consecutively known in the primitive days of Christian faith, whereas I believe Barth is right in his view that the threefoldness was given in the immediacy of what might be styled "the Palestinian moment." But Hodgson's refusal to confine revelatory and redemptive activity on God's part to that single event or series of events is most welcome.

Karl Barth rejects the *analogia entis* in its traditional form. That analogy, part of the general Catholic way of seeing things, began with the sheer fact of existence and the objects and experiences which are common and natural to men. From these it went on to attribute to God, eminently (or in a supreme degree), as the scholastics would say, those qualities which were found positively in the world. Thus to say that God is good is to say that our grasp of his goodness is not entirely contradictory to what we know of created or creaturely goodness, neither is it identical with such goodness; it is reflected in that goodness, but without the errors and limitations of the creature. Analogical statement is thus neither entirely negative nor entirely affirmative, although it tends to lean toward the latter. At the same time it has a negative quality, in that it denies that the created world is the exact and perfect replica of the divine life. Barth will have none of this; for him there is "no way from man to God," and our knowledge of God can come only from the divine side toward us.

Similarly Barth rejects the Augustinian teaching that there are *vestigia Trinitatis* in the created world. Augustine was prepared to say that in the world of nature and history, as well as in human experience, there are such "traces" of triunitarianism, although inevitably these are broken and partial. In respect to the way from man to God, Barth was ready to speak about "the analogy of grace" —that is, once man knows God through the divine self-revelation, it is possible to work back from that awareness, given by grace to faith, to something about God himself. In one way, this is a possible position, since only for those who have some sort of awareness of a clue or key to what God is up to can there be much sense in talking about what God is in himself through awareness of what he does in the creation. And Augustine himself would have argued that all genuinely "saving knowledge of God" depends upon there being, initially, some stance of faith, although that faith need not be the fully developed faith of the Christian in his response to the specific act of God in Jesus. For the African theologian, all human knowledge is made possible through a participation in the Word of God—a view which has Platonic antecedents; and we may speak of such participation as being in some sort a faithful and engraced matter.

But however this may be, it is my belief that there is an approach to triunitarian thought through an analysis of what might be called man's wider experiential awareness. In this and succeeding chapters we shall consider this approach. I wish to begin with a discussion of the way in which in human experience generally there is a sense of mystery, in which meaning is believed to be discovered as humankind makes a response to what is given in the happenings of nature and history and the concrete existence that we know so well.

Thomas Aquinas once wrote that "everything runs out into, or issues in, mystery" *(omnia abeunt in mysterium)*. In saying this, he once again demonstrated his profound insight into experience and the world in which that experience is had. While we must never "declare the mystery" too soon and by doing so succumb to all manner of superstition or esoteric nonsense, the fact remains that in any aspect of existence, once we have explored it as fully as we can, there is an element of the "given" (as von Hügel styled it) which is not explicable in terms of human ratiocinative skill. There is a "more" which must be faced and accepted; and this with what Wordsworth once called "natural piety." We live in the midst of mystery, and we ourselves are participant in mystery.

One way of getting at this was suggested by the French dramatist and philosopher Gabriel Marcel. As is well known, Marcel said that there is a distinction between a problem and a mystery. A problem, he urged, is a puzzle that in principle can be solved. By observation and experiment, by the use of reasoning and concentration of thought, we can discover the answer. Once we have the information that is required, we are able to work our way to a solution. This may not be easy, of course; to solve problems demands the devoted and single-minded following of such truth as we possess, a readiness to experiment and test, a capacity to observe and study what is presented to us, and all the techniques which we can bring to bear upon the matter. And it may take a very long time before we come within sight of the answer. Nonetheless, in principle (as I have put it), a problem is something that can be resolved and an answer given which will satisfy our minds and fulfill the requirements of logic, rationality, coherence, consistency, and meaning.

But a mystery is different. A mystery presents us with ultimate questions, for the answering of which we have neither the requisite data nor the necessary techniques; a mystery is recognized for what it is and we must accept it for what it is. Why is there anything at all, rather than simply nothing? For what purpose does anything exist, once we have got beyond the utilitarian and pragmatic answers? When Bertrand Russell complained that the American philosopher John Dewey lacked what Russell styled "cosmic piety" in his eager assumption that experimental and instrumental procedures would find solutions for whatever confronts us, he was pointing to the recognition of a mystery in and beyond things which the sages of the human race have always recognized and before which they have shown humility.

The world, like our experience, presents us with many problems. Most of these we are in the way of learning to solve, and among others the scientist is the person who has done much to assist us in reaching the answers. But there is more to the world and more in our experience than that; the saints and sages, the poets and artists, and those who retain even in maturity a childlike awareness of things, have always known this to be true. Basically, religion in all its forms has been a response to the presence of such mystery; and however varied may be the ways in which the response is made in different cultures, by different races, and at different times, nobody who is aware of the richness of human experience can deny that without such recognition, and the response it receives, human life is impoverished, cheapened, and made superficial and trivial.

Of course there are many who dislike this fact of mystery in things. They would prefer a Cartesian world, in which "clear and distinct ideas" can provide answers to everything, once we have managed to work out such a rational scheme. These are the people who overintellectualize, who fail to see the "aesthetic component" in experience, to use Prof. F. C. S. Northrop's telling phrase. Perhaps one of the defects of the Western world has been its easy succumbing to such an overintellectualizing, with the assumption that given time and effort we can work out an entirely rational explanation of everything. The Asian cultures, Northrop has remarked, have been much more ready to see the significance of deep "feeling tones," appreciation, judgments of value, and the recognition of profound mystery. This is why, in his judgment, we of the West are greatly in need of an infusion of that "aesthetic" awareness which will help to balance our too highly sophisticated trust in the deliverance of reason. I believe that Northrop has made a point which should receive our careful attention, for human existence and the world we experience and observe is indeed marked by great mystery.

We may take our human relationships as an excellent example of mystery. Obviously there is a considerable amount of useful problem-solving in respect to them. It is important to know something about others with whom we are associated, in their physiological, psychological, and sociological aspects. All human beings are psychosomatic organisms, with a physical structure, with the cells which make up our bodies, with the various systems (nervous, digestive, reproductive, etc.) which are ours, with a brain and its neurological functioning, with whatever may be known about our emotional lives and about our intelligence, with our possible and actual relationships in family, neighborhood, community, and nation. Each of these areas, and others too, may be observed and studied; reports may be given on the basis of such investigation and predictions may be made about probable patterns of behavior. But when all this is accomplished—and anything like an exhaustive account of human existence as thus constituting a problem to be solved is very far from having been achieved, even in our own day of specialization and detailed inquiry—something remains. What is that remainder? Very simply put, it is the deep reality of the human relationship itself as we know and experience it.

One's relationship with friend, wife, child, lover, will include elements or aspects which are susceptible to physical, chemical, biological, psychological, and sociological investigation. But he or she is not merely a complicated equation to be worked out, a complex structure of cells to be observed, a collection of emotions, desires, or drives about which we may make significant reports. As each of us knows, the relationship is so profoundly personal, so inclusive and all-embracing in its concern, so much a matter of two "elusive 'I's' " meeting and in some fashion getting aboard one another's very existence, that it cannot be other than mysterious. You are you; the other is he or she; the meeting of you and that other is precisely that meeting and not another meeting, involving so much of the strange selfhood that is proper to each. Perhaps only the lover, the friend, the poet or artist or seer can grasp the true significance of the meeting; and even then that significance can be expressed only in allusive language, for it breaks through the words we use and speaks from, as well as to, the hidden depths of human selfhood-in-community.

There is an old saying about love: "Why do I love you? I can count a thousand ways; but chiefly I love you just because you are *you.*" Certainly there is an element of mystery which is inescapable and which brings a wonder, a joy, and a pathos to all sharing of life in love.

Or look at the fabric of the universe. We understand a good deal about it; we can explain parts of it and something of how it works. We can speak about the "laws of nature," by which we mean the observable regularities which make a reasonable degree of prediction possible. Scientists in many different fields of study have accomplished more than our ancestors could have guessed; the amount of knowledge which we now possess is simply enormous. New data are continually being brought to our attention. Nobody should think for a moment that problemsolving is at an end; perhaps it is only beginning. And we have every reason to welcome all the answers which are available to us.

On the other hand, the great questions remain, and they pose to us a mystery which is not of the same type as the problems with which scientists are concerned. Why is the world there at all? Why is it cosmos and not sheer chaos, utterly anarchic and senseless? What meaning does it possess, or is it completely without meaning? Questions of that order cannot be treated as if they were merely complicated ways of putting problems that are to be solved by further inquiry, observation, or experiment. Here is mystery, and the wise individual recognizes it for what it is.

I happen to live and work in a great university. Many of my colleagues and friends are distinguished scientists, some of them Nobel prizewinners and all of them men and women of integrity, honesty, and devotion. I notice that these men and women are very much aware of the mystery in things. I am not saying that they are "religious" in any conventional sense of that word; perhaps most of them are not, for often they are in reaction from a kind of religious teaching which "put them off" formal institutional religious bodies and have been alienated by what they take to be—whether they are right or wrong about this is another matter—the tendency of conventionally "religious" people to "declare the mystery too soon," about which I have already warned, or to be obdurate in their rejection of or indifference to the work of the scientist.

Yet these men and women are humble people, unlike those others (who might be called camp followers of science) who sometimes claim to have all the answers ready to hand or to be pretty sure of discovering those answers before very long. I say with complete confidence that the really great scientists whom I know or have known in the past show reverence for mystery and a humility before the cosmos which is often much more impressive than some of those who talk as if they had in their religious allegiance a neat pattern of things. These scientists work with great energy to solve the particular problems which they face; they do not deny but rather they recognize mystery where mystery confronts them.

Although I have just written critically of certain kinds of religion, I should wish to insist on the fact of the religious vision, in all cultures known to us, and with that vision a sense of mystery about human life and the world. This is often called awareness of the *sacred* or the *nu-*

minous, and from what anthropologists have told us we now know that reverence in the presence of mystery is universal, found even among primitive tribes which at first seemed to be lacking in it. At the moment I am not concerned to discuss the significance of this awe at the sacredness of life and of aspects of nature; we shall have something to say about this in the latter part of the present chapter. At the moment it must simply be noted that men and women of all sorts, literate or illiterate, savage or civilized, appear to show just such an attitude, however they may work out its implications.

Throughout history, we may conclude, men and women have recognized the mystery in things and in themselves. They have been aware of "the more"; they have sought to come to terms with it; they have usually been humble before it. And they have sought to interpret it by the use of such concepts, notions, models, or values as they accepted.

At the beginning the mystery has most frequently been understood in terms of the manifestation of sheer power, and there are still many people who think in that way. But as time has gone on, prophets and saints, poets and artists, sages and seers, of most varied background and using diverse idiom, have spoken of the mystery as more adequately interpreted in terms of justice and goodness and eventually in terms of something that in many ways is even more mysterious and awe-inspiring: namely, love. It is fascinating to see how this alteration of outlook takes place in almost every culture and with almost every group known to us. The word love is a poor word, to be sure, for it can suggest sentimentality or shoddy emotion. But it can also mean strength in giving-and-receiving, mutuality, outgoing of self with courage and forgetfulness of self, and a positive goodness that is intense and entire. It is in *this* sense, not in the sense of mild benevolence, that the great leaders of the human race have used the word. Thus we may say that in many parts of the world love like this is taken to be the real meaning of the mystery in the world and in human experience. The mystery remains but it is now interpreted as possessed of a quality or character which speaks directly and impressively to the human heart and mind. Certainly it is not mere speculation, for it is based upon the plain fact that love represents, in almost all nations, cultures, races, classes, and people, the highest value which they know and cherish. It is an emergent from the world of nature and history; and to interpret the world without taking this very seriously would be to omit a datum that is obviously at hand. Nonetheless, there can be no doubt that any reading of meaning in the mystery is by an act of faith.

Faith, like love, is an ambiguous word. On the one hand, it can suggest nothing more than silly credulity and superstitious acceptance of views that have little if anything to commend them; on the other, it can mean a genuine adventure of our spirit, in which we take the best that we have known and experienced and commit ourselves to this as worthy of our trust and confidence. In all genuine faith there is an element of doubt, as Paul Tillich used to say. That is, the faith is entertained against a background of mystery and with honest awareness that much may seem to tell against it. But *some* faith, in the sense of some commitment to what is taken to be the meaning present in and expressed through the mystery which surrounds us, is both natural and inevitable. Even if the faith is of a purely negative sort—to put it paradoxically, that the only meaning in the mystery is sheer meaninglessness or stupidity—there is still some commitment, demanding little or much of our allegiance, dedication, and readiness to act.

So we can look at words like those with which Thornton Wilder ended his novel *The Bridge of San Luis Rey:* "Love is the only survival, the only meaning." And we can ask ourselves whether that affirmation can conceivably be true. We shall never know, in an absolute sense, in this finite and limited world; that is the element of doubt. But we can commit ourselves, in trust and confidence, to its truth; that is the reality of faith. Nor does it lack at least some supporting evidence, so far as the experience of the race is concerned.

The story of humankind can be read in many different ways. One way of reading it was urged by Alfred North Whitehead, the founding father of the conceptuality known as Process Thought. In his great book *Adventures of Ideas* (New York: Cambridge University Press, 1933), Whitehead has this to say: "[Plato's] final conviction, towards the end of his life, [was] that the divine element in the world is to be conceived as a persuasive agency and not as a coercive agency" (p. 170). He goes on to claim that the story of human civilization is the history of the way in which this affirmation has increasingly been made by those who appealed to what he styles "all that is best in human nature." He proposes that the business of philosophical thought is "to provide a rational understanding of the rise of civilization [with just such a historical development], and of the tenderness [we can here supply love as a synonym] of . . . life itself, in a world which superficially is founded upon the clashings of senseless compulsion" (pp. 173–74). I believe that Whitehead is correct in his analysis of civilization's history and that he has properly expressed the purpose not only of philosophical thought, to which he refers, but of all profound thinking about the meaning of the mystery which the human race encounters in its experience of the world and in its introspective sense of its own existence. Although such wide agreement, granted different languages to express it, is not in itself a demonstration, it does provide some backing for the conviction that persuasion or love is the supreme expression of power; indeed, it is the focal expression of the mystery so far as it is given to the human mind and spirit to grasp it.

Despite the setbacks, deviations, distortions, denials, and rejections which are so patently visible in our world, despite the evil so inescapably to be seen in the physical, physiological, emotional, and moral realms, love may be our key word. This is no mere speculation; neither is it abstract theorizing. It is a faith which seems to have a universal appeal—and as civilizations become more rational and more morally ordered, they tend to put their stress just there. So we find in China a humble acceptance of the goodness of "heaven," however conceived, with profound consequences for the ordering of human life. We find in India a movement from the impersonal and abstract ground of all existence toward a commitment to goodness and compassion, whether in the teaching of the Bhagavad-Gita in Hinduism or the instructions which Gautama Buddha gave to his disciples. In Islam, the "names of God" begin with Allah's sheer omnipotence but move on to speak of him as "the Compassionate One." In Judaism, the development is obvious to anyone who reads the Bible in the proper order of its books, from the "Lord of hosts" who chiefly shows himself in natural catastrophe to the "Father of Israel" who is faithful, loving, and concerned.

Christians would wish to go beyond all this. They say—and I say as a Christian—that outgoing love has become a fact in history and of human experience; it has been given concrete expression, the Christian would affirm, in at least one fully human life, that of Jesus of Nazareth. In him, teaching about such love and his behavior which acted out such love has (Christians believe) found its embodiment in the Man who taught in this way and behaved in this way. He *is* the human enactment of the Love which is the meaning of the mystery, and the Love which ultimately he is has been given concrete human statement in a genuine instance of human loving. This remains a venture of faith; "we walk by faith, not by sight." But it has been verified in the experience of the millions who have been prepared to commit themselves to it and let it work through them in their ordinary lives and in the world of human affairs. Here is the specific Christian claim; here is the ground of specific Christian experience.

There is the circumambient mystery and there is the meaning of that mystery disclosed to us in the love which makes its urgent appeal to human beings everywhere, supremely and decisively (so Christians dare to say) in the Man of Nazareth. But to accept this, faith is required. A response must be made; and that response is through commitment and through the readiness to be conformed to the reality which is disclosed in the meaning of the mystery. This is the third element or aspect of the "experiential awareness," as I have entitled the present chapter. A triunitarian pattern is beginning to emerge.

The act of faith is plainly enough an act of men and women. They make it as a decision which is freely taken. Sometimes the decision is part of an almost overwhelming experience; sometimes it is a gradual growth in willingness to give oneself in trust and confidence. To deny the human aspect and to minimize the freedom which it presupposes is to turn people into robots or to subscribe to a determinism which denies to human agents any capacity to say yes or no to possibilities which are offered. Yet there is a sense in which the act of faith and the decision which it includes is not entirely a matter of human consent, as if one were able to decline it altogether or to refuse to make any choice at all. We can see something of this ambiguity in the experience of artists and poets, to take a fairly simple example.

Vincent van Gogh, the painter whose work has captivated so many in recent years, began his artistic activity among the potato pickers and the miners in Belgium. His early paintings have a strange, somber quality. But then he went to the south of France and lived in and near Arles. From that time his paintings changed; they were suffused with sunlight and danced with color. Van Gogh wrote about this to his brother Theo. He told Theo that when he got to southern France he felt the sun so strongly that he "had to paint" in this new fashion. Certainly there was his own decision; one might almost say that he chose to "commit" himself to the brilliant light of the countryside around Arles. At the same time there was a compulsion upon him to paint as he now did. He did not feel that he was lacking freedom in doing so; he was only aware of a pressure, exercised forcibly in a way but also felt persuasively, to put on canvas what he was feeling, experiencing, enjoying.

Or take D. H. Lawrence, who once wrote about his poetry that it was written not so much by him as "by the wind that blows through me." He was the instrument for that "wind," so to say; he was also free to decide whether or not he would permit the "wind" to possess him and use him. I have quoted these two examples in other books and I apologize for repeating them here, but I believe that they are relevant to our main theme. That theme is the double character of response made to what lures, attracts, and entices us. On the one hand, we are conscious that it is we ourselves who make the response; on the other hand, we are in the presence of and find ourselves caught up in a response which extends beyond our human capacity.

So it is when we "fall in love," as we say. There is a mystery here, as I have urged earlier in this chapter. But there is also disclosure on the part of the other. The other says or does something, or in some fashion makes an impression upon us. There is an attraction or appeal which speaks to us in the very depths of our being. Certainly we could quite easily say no to that attraction or appeal; we could turn our attention elsewhere. To that degree and in that sense we are entirely free to decide. Yet we are so strongly attracted, by whatever it is which has made its appeal, we may feel impelled to say yes; in saying it we are conscious that, far from denying or rejecting the freedom which is proper to us in making a decision, we have in truth experienced a great liberation. Augustine spoke out of his own experience when he said that this is the greater liberty (*libertas major*), in comparison with which merely psychological indeterminism, in its customary sense of ability to say no and yes in an indifferent manner, is only a very minor freedom (*libertas minor*). Aristotle too had insight into this truth in his speaking about "the power" which the beloved can exercise over the lover, yet without negating the lover's freedom as a human being.

Now it is my contention that in the response which is made by the venture of faith to the disclosure of mystery's meaning, such as the great ones of the human race have so insistently proclaimed, we have this same sort of duality. Paul spoke as a believer in Christ when he said of his own action, "Not I, but Christ who dwelleth in me." But even as he said this, he was quite aware of his own responsible freedom, for as he wrote elsewhere, we must "work out our own salvation with fear and trembling," while yet "it is God who worketh in me. . . ." This specifically religious and Christian example makes the point very aptly indeed. And so it is with all deep response in the commitment which is faith to the meaning which we believe to have been declared to us out of the mystery in which we live and which surrounds us on every side. Here is a third, to complete the triunitarian pattern of experience: the response, the meaning found or discovered but in the last resort accepted as given, and the mystery from which both meaning and response proceed and in which they have their origin. To deny any one of them is to impoverish the experience or to dismiss one or another of the data which the experience entails.

In discussing the theology of Karl Barth I criticized this distinguished Swiss thinker for his excessive christocentrism. I pointed out that in the Patristic Age there was a readiness to welcome hospitably whatever men and women, in any place and at any time, had done which was good or true or just or loving. Somehow or other, the Fathers (with the exception of Tertullian) were prepared to allow, God had nowhere left himself without witness, as Paul put it. Or, as Augustine said, there are *vestigia Trinitatis*, traces of the triune God's presence and activity, in all human experience and in the world which we observe. This generous recognition of non-Christian and even nonreligious disclosure of God provided the setting for and the context of the Christian affirmation about Jesus Christ. He was distinctive, decisive, normative, definitive—call it what you will— but he was not removed from, nor was he alien to, the ordinary ways in which response was made by men and women, and supremely men and women of insight and humility like (for the Fathers) a Socrates or a Plato and, we should wish to add, others like the Buddha, the writer of the

Bhagavad-Gita, even a Confucius. All these were caught up into and used by God as he worked for and with his human children. The speciality attaching to Jesus was that in him, in a fashion which seemed to the Fathers unmistakable and vivid, a clue or key had been given. By the use of that key and following that clue it was then possible to "test" what elsewhere seemed to have been disclosed. This is the true significance of the phrase so often used in recent theology, "the finality of Christ." It is not the sort of uniqueness which is without any comparisons, parallels, approximations, or adumbrations; it is a speciality which is given in the vital and vivid quality of his disclosure and the consequent freedom which is granted to humankind, once it responds to that disclosure.

We may put this in the language which has been used in the present chapter. The meaning of the mystery in creation and in human life is nothing other than the "pure unbounded love" which is given signal expression in Jesus. The response that is made in faith, with utter trust and confidence, to that signal expression is distinctive and special too. But from one point of view, the importance of the disclosure and the response to it is in its opening to us all a way of seeing and a way of living which can find room for whatever else is good or true or lovely or just. And one helpful way of proceeding is to begin with that broader awareness, seeing that humankind because of its very humanity seeks and thinks it finds meaning present in the mystery and responds to it with greater or less readiness to commit the self to that meaning. If you will allow this phrasing, we have here an analogue to God's triunity.

The analogue of mystery-meaning-understanding is but one of many possible intimations of the divine triunity, however. I have dwelt upon it because, to my knowledge, this is the first attempt to develop it for theological purposes. Its special value is that it seems to combine both the personal and social approaches to the doctrine of God. There is an evident unitary quality in the complex experience of responding to meaning given to the mystery in which we live; at the same time there is a threefoldness in the distinctions among the terms understanding, meaning, and experienced mystery. More particularly, when in this chapter I have spoken of the reality and relationships in our experience of love, something like Augustine's suggestion of its usefulness as an analogy is obviously present. Although he himself uses the analogy of love on only one occasion in his great work *De Trinitate* and is more insistent on a psychological analogy, the African doctor was certainly right in his more general emphasis on God as primarily to be thought of in terms of love. He comes back to this in almost all his postconversion writing, even if his neo-Platonic background, with its stress on being, also reappears from time to time, and even if with his own experience of moral struggle (as well as his dependence upon scriptural texts) he is ready to speak of divine will.

There are many other possible analogies of a triunitarian sort, in secular life as well as in human experience generally. I shall mention only one of these, suggested by Dorothy Sayers in her notable book *The Mind of the Maker*, published many years ago. Miss Sayers was a novelist, a poet, and an amateur theologian of no little ability. From her own knowledge of the work of an author, she sought to show how there is a threefold unity in the writing of a story. The author has an idea in mind which will provide the theme for a book; obviously this idea—shall we speak of the plot of the novel?—has a certain priority, since in our temporal world there is a necessary successiveness in all activity. But the writer must then express the idea in some form or other. The actual development of this initial idea in the writing of the story is the second essential aspect of his or her literary activity. And then there is the completed tale, as it fulfills (or fails to fulfill) the intention of the author in writing it; and along with this comes the way in which readers, on their part, respond to the material which does thus express, to greater or less degree, the initial idea in the novelist's mind. We have here both a unity and a diversity; and the chronological succession with its threefoldness is perhaps not so significant as the union which is in fact present in "the mind of the maker." Not so significant, however, in one sense only: that successive development is posterior to the total vision of the writer, which includes within it the original idea, the possibility of setting it out in the actual putting of pen on paper, and the likelihood that there will be a genuine fulfillment of the intention in what is, in fact, set down. Interestingly enough, the title of Miss Sayers' book has a double meaning. The word maker is the old term for a poet as well as for someone who "makes" something in our modern sense. Her purpose was to point toward a genuine analogy to triunitarianism in the activity of the aesthetic genius; to my mind the analogy might well be extended to all high artistic effort.

None of these analogies is final and conclusive. The most that we can expect of *any* analogy is that it will point toward what is beyond itself; furthermore, in using an analogy we must always allow for its imperfection and for the certainty that in the finitude which attaches to it there will be some inadequacy, perhaps even a suggestion of presumed consequences that need negation. But we cannot get along without analogies when we are talking of God. He is not present to us for examination; he is not to be "observed" in any clear and precise fashion. Hence he must be *pointed to*, not defined. This is where analogy comes to our aid.

Finally, let us observe that the Fathers themselves used this sort of analogical talk. When Origen spoke of the sun, its rays of light, and the illumination and warmth it produced, and sought to apply this three-in-oneness to the doctrine of God as triune, he was speaking analogically. So also with the psychological and social analogies of Augustine; and the same is true of the Cappadocians with their platonizing use of concepts of being and their example of "the three men" (Peter, James, and John) to which usage we have already referred, who are yet one in the "form" of manhood as it is individuated in this and that instance.

The difficulty with the theology which we have inherited, some of us think, is to be found somewhere else: that traditional theology, commonly called "orthodox," has been guilty time and again, without realizing what was taking place, of taking *being* in an abstract sense, conceived as perfect in changelessness and lack of relationships, or alternatively of stressing power in a highly coercive sense, as the key to the divine reality. This has resulted in a system of Christian thought in which God as Love or Lover has only an adjectival place—certainly an apostasy from the "Galilean vision," as Whitehead called the event of Christ in its full reality. To say "God" ought to be to say "Love." God in his creative fatherhood *is* Love; God in his self-expressive activity *is* Love; God as enabling response to that activity *is* Love. This is the deepest Christian insight, spelled out in a triunitarian way. And yet, to paraphrase the *Quicunque Vult*, "there are not three Loves but one Love"— God himself, who *is* Love.

4
Contemporary Understanding

In what used to be called philosophy of religion and nowadays is often styled philosophical theology, it has been customary to speak of God as transcendent and as immanent—above the world and in the world, as we often put it. So too it has been customary to refer to God "as he is in himself" and to God "as he acts in the world" or "as he reveals himself in the world." In each case we have a twofold distinction, one which might be put in yet another way by talking of God taken to be remote from the creation and of God as in some fashion present in the creation.

This double fashion of speaking about God is found in a very interesting little book by Prof. Cyril C. Richardson of Union Theological Seminary in New York, published under the title *The Doctrine of the Trinity* (Nashville, Tenn.: Abingdon, 1958). Its author is a learned patristics scholar, and he writes with vast knowledge of early Christian thinking. His contention is that the traditional triunitarian teaching about God will not stand up to logical analysis because it adds what might be called "a third dimension" to the two with which we began this chapter: God as totally other than the world and God as active and revealed in the world. Dr. Richardson contends also that there is no genuine distinction in scriptural material between the work of the Logos, Word, Wisdom, or Son, on the one hand, and the Holy Spirit on the other. Everything said about these really comes down to talk about God's activity or his revelation in the creation; the only difference is a terminological one. He does not propose that we jettison the traditional symbolism of Father, Son or Word, and Holy Spirit; rather, in his view, we should retain this precisely *as* symbolism, valuable in worship and devotion, but we should not attempt to maintain the necessity of the triunitarian theology as such.

Other modern writers have sometimes written in the same fashion, but perhaps none with the learning, clarity, and deep religious feeling shown in Professor Richardson's little book. I am not willing to accept his position, however, and my rejection of it is based on several grounds.

In the first place, I am not convinced that the scriptural terminology is clearly on his side. Naturally there is a very considerable variety of language, especially in the Old Testament, when writers are talking about God's way of acting in and of revealing himself to the world. It is not easy to distribute the names for this activity in a precise fashion, so there are many ambiguities. But I think, on the other hand, that back of the terminological confusion (as it often is) there is a genuine distinction between God as he declares himself *to men and women* and God as he works *with the creation,* in the first instance; and God as he *enables and inspires* a recognition of this revelation and working. "The Word of God came to me," in the first case; "I was taught by the Spirit," in the second. If we wish to stress the action of God in the life of the people of Israel, then the events which happened in the course of their existence, whether among them in their national life or upon them through other peoples or through the natural order, are not simply identical with the way in which that communal life does, or does not, conform itself to God's will declared through such events; nor is it the same as the way in which through such conformity or lack of it the life of the people is thought to be faithful in dedication and commitment to its calling. The language may be confused and confusing, but the duality seems to me to be genuinely present in the midst of that very confusion.

I have entitled this chapter Contemporary Understanding because I believe that we see in other writers of our time *and* in much that is thought and said by Christian believers today a recognition that the twofold distinction is not adequate and that it is necessary to speak of three, not just two, aspects or modes or ways in which we may refer to God. This third I myself should wish to style the divine concomitance with the creation, distinguishing it from, yet relating it always with, the divine transcendence and the divine immanence. Or, to use the other conventional distinction, which speaks of "God as he is in himself" and "God as he acts in or reveals himself to the world," I believe that we may add "God as he evokes and enables the world to make its due response or answer to his working and revelation." I have already written along these lines in the earlier chapters of this book, and I shall return to that emphasis as we proceed. Here I wish to indicate that the threefoldness has been seen for what it is, within Christian circles at least, thanks to two important developments. One is the renewed study of scripture, in which (*pace* Dr. Richardson) there is considerable discussion of the ways in which the Bible does in fact talk about the Word or Wisdom of God, on the one hand, and the Spirit of God, on the other. The second development is to be found in the quite remarkable revival of interest in the Holy Spirit in our own time, not only in the charismatic and pentecostal movements but within more traditional and established Christian communions. To my mind, this revival of interest, with its resultant emphasis on "Spirit possession" in the Christian fellowship—whether by more extreme expressions in the sectarian groups or by renewed awareness in the mainstream churches of the work of the Spirit in Christian life, worship, sacraments, prayer, etc.—has made its own implicit criticism of failure to find a "third" among the modes of divine being and activity in the world and among men and women.

There is a third point to which attention should also be drawn. This is the influence upon philosophical theology of the central Christian declaration that in

Christ God is incarnate in human existence and the corollary of this declaration (found in the ancient Fathers) in the conviction that the Word who was incarnate there in that historical event is the same Word that has been present in and active through the creation from the beginning, providing a context for the specific action of God in that particular place and time. In other words, much contemporary philosophical theology is taking very seriously, perhaps almost for the first time in the history of Christian thought, the illumination which the incarnation in Jesus may throw upon the rest of the divine operation in the world. For if the Incarnation is indeed regarded with utmost seriousness in its illuminating of "how things go in the world" and not simply taken as a statement which must be made about the Man Jesus and his (so to say) "personal" significance, it carries with it quite important consequences.

Thus, I have suggested that the *tertium quid* between transcendence and immanence is concomitance—and I am using this word as a practical equivalent of incarnation. If in Jesus Christ God is concomitant with men, does not this indicate that in some way or other we should claim that God is also concomitant with the whole creation, once the divine action in Jesus is asserted to be the action of the Word about whom the first part of the first chapter of John's Gospel speaks? Or, to put it in another way, if in Jesus God has willed to become the companion of his children, does not this suggest, even require, a companionship of God not only with all men and women at every time and place but also with his whole creation? Should this be true, then we must speak of God as not only the originative and creative principle behind and "above" the world, not only of God as working in that world, but of that working as being twofold in its operation. God is the sharer in and companion of the creation, in the first place; and God is active in the inner life and responsive movement through the world, in the second. It is my contention that our renewed awareness of the Holy Spirit, as well as our finding in the Incarnation what might well be styled a metaphysical principle, makes it necessary for us to say exactly this.

I wish now to consider, in the light of the points just made, a possible contemporary understanding of the reality of God which can go beyond the usual "in himself" and "as he works" distinction and the usual transcendence-immanence distinction. Such a contemporary view may very well be useful theologically, as I am sure it is; it may also have much to contribute to practical religion as men and women experience it.

We live in a world which does not explain itself. By this I mean that the ultimate reason for there being a world at all cannot be found from within the world, since the best that we can manage is the handling of problems in this or that area, the attempt at a description of how things work in limited aspects of the creation, and the proposal that in this or that fashion there are such regularities of behavior as would enable a degree of prediction in consequence of already observed patterns. But the great "why" questions always require some sort of extrapolation from the experienced or observed phenomena which are open to our study and report. This is why in all parts of the civilized world there has been talk about a "first cause" which might provide the final answer to our question of "why." In many different ways, not only among religious people but also in philosophical discussion, something like a primal causative principle has been asserted. Whatever may be the mode of argument and however varied may be the language which is used, there is a general agreement that there must be some source or origin for the whole cosmos.

Unfortunately our finite minds are not competent to arrive at a description of such a source or origin. We are able only to reach a description of this or that particular area or aspect which is open to our study, although of course the things we say are open to revision in the light of newer information made available to us in the realm of scientific inquiry as investigation proceeds, further experiments are undertaken, and data are recognized that previously had not been known. Beyond this realm in its finitude we do not seem able to go, certainly so far as descriptive statements are concerned. That there is some source or origin appears to be accepted by almost everybody, save those who rest content in what they would call agnosticism. That is, there are those who simply refuse to move beyond the world of phenomena and prefer to rest in a condition of nescience: no clear knowledge, therefore no attempt to make statements beyond those possible through experiment, observation, and human experience.

But two points may be made here. First, it is possible that there is more in human experience than is phenomenally explicable. Here the testimony of saints and mystics, and many ordinary people too, tells us that for them at least there is an experience which has brought them into contact, as they believe, with what is beyond or above the world as such. Second, that in all profound philosophical and religious discourse, whatever may be the case with superficial thinking, there is always an element of agnosticism. That is to say, there is always the mystery about which we spoke in the last chapter, and only a fool would claim to possess full and complete knowledge, if knowledge there is, of the source or origin of things.

But if source or origin there be, it may perhaps be *pointed to*, even though it cannot be defined or described with exact, precise, and completely exhaustive accuracy. In many parts of the world, perhaps more especially in those which have been influenced by the thinking of the Greek philosophers, it has been thought that something of the nature of the source or origin of all things must be expressed in the things themselves. The "first cause," it is said, precisely *because* it is primally causative, may be understood in part through the things that we know and see in the world in which we live. Thus the religious seers have spoken of the Creator who is manifest in his creation. Because the creation is finite, the manifestation will be partial at best and distorted at worst; none the less it will be there, since no "maker" can engage in work without leaving some traces of himself in that which he does.

So it is that the view has been advanced that in a mysterious way the origin or source is expressed in the creation—there is the possibility of reading up from the creation to the Creator, provided this is done in all humility and with full recognition of the partial and imperfect character of all such reading. If there is any trace of purpose in the world, for example, this may be taken to indicate that there is a supreme purpose in the origin or source; there has been some divine intention which is behind and beyond those instances of purpose which we can see about us. These two lines of thought—arguing from the world to its origin or source, and reading something of the nature of that source from the world—have commonly been called by philosophers the cosmological and teleological arguments. The former has to do with predicating or asserting a necessary cause for the existence of a world at all, with all its chains of "secondary" or observable causation; the latter has to do with the presence of some purposive intention in that cause, as an explanation of the facts of development toward goals and the adaptation of means to ends which seem to be given in our experience.

There have been further claims, however. As I have just said, many millions of people, including some of the wisest of the human race, have been prepared to speak of a sense of an other than themselves, of which they are aware at exalted moments of experience. The fact of religious experience, to give this its usual name, has been so persistent that a thinker like Whitehead regarded it as one of the inescapable data with which any responsible philosopher must deal, although the philosopher may not possess that religious sense in any marked degree or indeed may never have known it in his or her own life. This sense of an other, however defined or described, has been a source of what Whitehead called "refreshment" and "companionship." In moments of disillusion and despair, in times of worry and fear, it seems that there may be a "refreshment" (to use Whitehead's term) which strengthens, encourages, and enlightens those to whom it comes. And at the same time, there is a presence which provides a "companionship" in life's activity that redeems it from triviality and provides for those who possess it an awareness that they are not entirely alone in their struggle to live well—or, indeed, to live at all. Sometimes this companionship, this sense of presence, is pictured in personalistic terms; sometimes it appears to be taken as more like a force or power of an impersonal nature. In the Jewish-Christian tradition, personal language has been used about it; in the Eastern cultures, as for example in much of earlier Hinduism and in Buddhism, more impersonal ways of speaking have prevailed. In Chinese thought, the awareness has been commonly taken to be "the presence of Heaven," with no description offered and certainly without personalizing definition. None the less, this kind of experience is so nearly universal that it may very well be regarded as natural to the human race as such.

In the attempt of philosophers of religion to work out a scheme which will account for the two—the conviction that there must be a supracreaturely source or origin, and the assurance that the experience of refreshment and companionship is both real and indicative of a "more than man" and a "more than the world"—one of the developments has been by way of saying that precisely in the feeling of companionship, with its result in strengthening or refreshing, there is a genuine expression of the source or origin of the world. There is also the belief that when and as men and women make an effort to conform to the best and highest they know, a genuine response is made to the source or origin which has expressed itself to them in their religious awareness. This is why spiritual disciplines, rules of life, guidelines for behavior, and the like have been devised in all religious cultures. The purpose of these is to enable human beings so to adjust themselves to the reality of things, at a level more profound than that of mere appearance in the world of phenomenal observation, that they may grow more perceptive and may more readily be attuned to the expression of that reality in their day-by-day existence.

Subjectively, then, they may be led to life in relationship with the source, the origin, the primal causative agency, finding their efforts strengthened as they seek to do this; and at the same time having some awareness, mostly dim but on occasion vivid and compelling, that they are not alone in their existence but rather have with them a presence that answers their need. The presence, they would say, is objectively *there*; but it cannot be rightly experienced, nor the strengthening or refreshment it gives adequately received, unless they make their subjective response to what is given.

This scheme has often been given theological, and in many quarters also philosophical, statement in talk about a transcendent which is immanent. That is, beyond and above the world there is a reality which exists in and of itself, but a reality which is also in and with the world. It seems to me that this common manner of putting the case is too simple, however. It lumps together, under the word immanent, what are really two diverse modes of the transcendent's presence in and action through the created order. As I have urged earlier, a *third* term seems to me required here, and I have suggested "concomitance" to supplement the usual pairing together of transcendence and immanence. This term is practically synonymous with "incarnation"; and I have contended, and believe, that one of the reasons for a growing awareness of such a "third" is the fashion in which incarnational thought has become fairly widespread in many Christian circles.

Perhaps another reason is that suggested by Whitehead in his chapter on "The New Reformation" in *Adventures of Ideas* (to which reference has already been made): the great contribution made by certain thinkers of the Patristic Age, particularly those who worked in Alexandria, in their attempt to find a way in which God understood as transcendent could be seen to be at work in the created world. The patristic stress to which Whitehead turned was not upon divine immanence as this notion was related to the Holy Spirit. Rather, it was upon the Logos or Word of God. The fathers of the ancient church put their emphasis on the specific instance of the incarnation of God the Logos in Jesus. Whitehead and others who share a wider view of incarnational activity in the world are more interested in the fashion in which what these Fathers said about Jesus Christ may also be said about God's activity in the world as incarnational in quality—and this without questioning the meaningfulness of immanence as a different, but related, mode of divine operation.

Following this line of thought, it might then be said that God the Father is appropriately styled "transcendent," or God as he is in himself alone, God the Holy Ghost "immanent," and God the Logos or Word "concomitant" or "incarnate." I have said "appropriately"; by this I mean that certain functions of deity may be appropriated to the several distinctions. Something of this sort has indeed been customary in Western Christian theology. Unoriginate transcendence is spoken of the Father; creative and redemptive activity is spoken of the Word; and inspiration is spoken of the Holy Spirit. But this manner of speech fails on several counts.

First, it does not sufficiently grasp the point made by Augustine: *all* three distinctions are present in that which any one of them may be said to do. If all God's working *ad extra* is "indivisible" *(indivisa)*, we may conclude that the three modes of divine being are also the divine modes of activity, inseparable, mutually indwelling, and reciprocal in their relations. A further problem, however, is the failure to see the truth in Karl Barth's argument that God's being *is* his activity—or to put the same point in the language common among Process theologians, a thing *is* what it does: God *is* his activity. Hence we need to look more carefully at the kind of theology which is prepared to speak of "God in and of himself" *and* of "God in his activity in the world." Can that kind of speech be maintained? I believe not.

The type of thinking behind this kind of discussion is Hellenistic, with its talk about substance as almost a "thing in itself" apart from its behavior or working. If we give up that type of thinking and elect to use the language of more contemporary science and thought, we cannot meaningfully separate any entities from their operations. We cannot talk about an entity as if it were rather like a clothesline upon which Monday's wash—experiences, actions, workings—may be hung. On the contrary, to speak meaningfully in our day is to talk of events or happenings, of occurrences or occasions. At the same time we must understand the societal nature of the world, where each and every event or happening influences and is influenced by every other event or happening. Nothing exists in and of itself. And unless God is the complete contradiction of the world in which he is said to be at work, he must have his existence in what he does; while what he is, as being present in what he does, is never properly understood independently of that with which he is related—and which he both effects and is affected by.

In other words, we are back in the position of ancient Hebrew thought as expressed in the Jewish scriptures. We can now talk of the living God, whose nature was stated in the famous words from Exodus: "I shall be doing what I shall be doing" or "I shall reveal myself in what I reveal myself to be doing." That famous text is mistranslated in most English versions of the Old Testament, where it is taken to mean "I am what I am." The difficulty in that way of putting it is that the Hebrew tongue, when speaking of a present, always implies a future—this is the familiar eschatological view which runs through Jewish thought. But the difficulty is also in the failure of the translators of the usual version to recognize the vitalistic or living nature of God as the Jew understood him. For the Jew the mystery of the world was not a hiding of deity in self-contained and unrelational reality, but the mystery in the divine activity or purpose movement in the world and behind the world. If God "hides himself," as the Jew knew quite well he did, it is not in some substantial selfhood but in the mysterious way in which he acted, genuinely and historically but yet without exhausting himself in his action in the world. There is always "more" which God can do and which in his working he most certainly will do.

One of the distinctive characteristics of Jewish thought as the scriptures reflect it is an unwillingness to speak about God apart from his working in the world. Nor was this only another aspect of that reverence which made it seem blasphemous to use the divine name in their speech. Rather, it was their vivid sense of the livingness of God, his ceaseless and faithful action in the world of nature and in history; this made it impossible for them to think that behind those acts there was a reality which was entirely unrelated with and essentially unconcerned for the creation. Of course there was a mystery in God; he was unexhausted (and inexhaustible) in his work in the creation. Yet for them, if I may put it in this way, God most certainly *was* what God *did*—in the phrase I have used a few paragraphs back. His modes of activity were diverse, to be sure: he was creative and creating, he was redeeming and revealing, he was inspiring and enabling ("refreshing" would be a good word here). But because they were not interested in metaphysical speculation after the fashion which was followed by the Greeks and other ancient peoples, but were concerned primarily with seeing what things were in terms of the way in which those things were worked out, they did not indulge in theories about an unmoved mover or an eternally subsistent entity or substance or even about an abstract "first cause." They preferred to talk about what was going on in nature and history. Obviously they attributed the "going on" ultimately to an effecting of God's will and a realization of his purpose. Their language was more realistic and concrete because that also was the fashion in which they both lived and thought. Nor is it accidental that they used an idiom which was poetic—metaphor and simile, image and picture—in its character. The reason for this, I believe, is that only by the use of language of that sort is it possible to point to and talk about events or happenings.

A consequence is that when the Jewish scriptures do in fact make assertions which to us have ontological reference—that is, are pointers to the true nature of things and their abiding reality—they speak in non-speculative idiom. They do not say that God is transcendent; rather, they speak of him "as high and lifted up." And so with other assertions that in the abstract idiom of Hellenistic philosophy would have been phrased in strictly conceptual terms. All this is relevant to our main topic, since it indicates that an imaginative and hence pictorial way of seeing things can bring us to some deeper understanding of what triunitarian faith is about. As G. K. Chesterton once said, "Never believe in anything that can't be told in painted pictures." That is how the Jews did the job.

I have spoken of the influence of incarnationalism, which has been one of the reasons for insisting on a "third" in the modes of divine activity and hence of the divine life. In the long years when "biblical theology" was taken as if it alone could be the ground for Christian thought, there was considerable attack on "incarnationalism," as well as on the sacramentalist interpretation of the creation as a whole. It was contended that neither of these terms is present in scripture, which is of course true enough, and it was further claimed that a soundly based theology with its point of reference in the Bible could not allow for such "philosophizing" readings of the world. Of course this attack was mounted, for the most part, by those who treated the Bible as if it could be read in isolation both from influences that played upon its writers and also from reasonable consequences of the scriptural data when these were taken as providing a key or clue to wider understanding of the realms of experience, history, and nature. Now that this excessive biblicism has ceased to dominate the world of theology and the possibility of a genuinely constructive philosophical theology has increasingly been accepted, there is no need to feel uncomfortable when views that are not specifically biblical, but are based upon a reading of the significance of biblical material, are proposed. I believe that this is coming to be recognized in respect to incarnationalism and sacramentalism—in other words, to the possibility of the concomitance of God with his creation, to fill out the picture of God as transcendent to but never unrelated with the creation, and God as immanently working in and through it to secure a response to his action on and with it.

In the contemporary rediscovery of the doctrine of the Holy Spirit, however, we have one valuable result of the period during which scripture received such intensive, if also overexclusive, attention. Study of scripture is not, obviously, the only source for the charismatic or pentecostal revival of our own day. Acknowledgment must be made of the concrete deliverance of experience as men and women have been impelled to recognize the presence and power of the living Christ upon their lives and in consequence have become aware of a powerful yet persuasive working through them which exceeds any purely human movement and which also goes beyond what ordinary psychology of religion might easily have accounted for.

The experience of those who have felt this strong working of the Holy Spirit in their lives goes far to establish the distinction between Word, or revelatory and redemptive act of God, *and* response in faith and commitment. While it would be a mistake, in my view, to press the distinction of subjective and objective too far in any discussion of human knowledge and experience, it remains the fact that there *is* a distinction between the given datum of the life, teaching, action, death, and resurrection of Christ as an event wrought out in the realm of history *and* the deeply felt evocation of faith in him, with commitment of life to him and the resultant awareness of new power and a growth in love within the fellowship of others who are also caught up in that faith. It has been customary in traditional theology to speak of faith as one of the "theological virtues," along with hope and love; these are not believed to be "worked up" by human effort but rather to be gifts of God to his children. Perhaps that way of phrasing the matter does not appeal to us, but there may be an insight here which is worth noticing and stating in a more suitable idiom. In any event, the experience of the Spirit as the enabler of response to the act of God in Christ, with a plain difference between the givenness of the act, on the one hand, and the response made to it, on the other, would seem to confirm the argument I have presented. What is more, it would seem to show the inadequacy of the type of binitarianism which is advocated for theological-philosophical purposes by those who talk only of God "in himself" and God "active in and revealed to the world," or of God as transcendent and God as immanent, and leave the matter there. There *is* a third, and it would be a grave mistake to deny that third in the interests of neatness or a simplistic reading of the biblical material.

I shall conclude this chapter by some discussion of the remarkable way in which a recognition of this threefoldness has its association with the increasingly familiar insistence that in human experience, as well as in the wider world of nature, we have to do with an essentially societal creation. We shall have occasion to return to this point in our later study; here I wish to remark upon the mutuality of influence or affect, in which every creaturely occurrence is related to and bound up with other such occurrences, wherever we turn. Now at the human level, of which we have firsthand knowledge, we are certainly aware of the personal and social as always found together. There is no personal existence which is not also a social existence. Men and women are not mere *individuals;* they are *persons*—and the difference is worth our stressing. An individual is defined in the dictionaries as one instance of a particular species, genus, or class. But as Thomas Aquinas saw long ago, human beings are more than that, since we are in necessary relationship with others of our race; we are personal, as Aquinas said, because we are open to influence by others and ourselves are influential upon them. Personal life is of enormous value, but so also is social life; the two belong together, and either without the other is less than the facts of experience present to us.

The triunitarian picture of God is a way of saying that in God the values of both the personal and social are guaranteed, as in God those values also have their source and ground. It might be possible to say this in a binitarian perspective, with its dual stress upon God as transcendent and as immanent or upon God as unoriginate source and as active in the world. As a matter of fact, however, the tendency of both these positions has been toward a view of God as in himself unrelated and even remote from the world, on the one hand, yet in some fashion willing and able to act upon and work in the creation, on the other. This gives little opportunity for a genuinely personal-social way of understanding his nature; it is more likely to result in a unitarianism of sorts, stressing so much either the completeness of God in himself or his action in the world that the one not stressed is likely to be minimized or reduced to a second place.

A full-orbed triunitarian conception, however, when combined with the Barthian insight that God is as God acts—something *is* what it *does*—readily provides a background and guarantee for a richly personal-social picture of deity, as it also validates in a vivid fashion the concrete human experience of personal existence as always set in a social context.

In our next chapter we shall move on to consider some other points which have frequently been forgotten in talk about God's nature and activity in creation. These have to do with the way in which a triunitarian conception of the divine reality includes what is of significance in deism, humanism, and spiritism, any one of which when taken by itself leads in the end to virtual atheism, whether theoretical or practical. We shall also have occasion to argue that a genuine theism is essentially *pan-en-theism*, to employ a word coined by the German thinker K. C. F. Krause in the last century and used again in this one by Baron Friedrich von Hügel and Prof. Charles Hartshorne. The discussion will lead directly to the effort, made in the last chapter of this book, to show that the conceptuality known as Process Thought—so influential in North America today and more and more respected in Britain and elsewhere, even by those who do not feel inclined to accept it for themselves—may be of considerable assistance to us in re-thinking or re-conceiving the inherited conviction of the Christian church that God is no singular monad but in some profound sense is triunitarianism in his nature because he is triune in his action in the creation.

5
The
Inclusive
Reality

In the philosophy of religion as it has developed over the centuries there are several different ideas or concepts of God. One is the idea of God as onetime creator of the world, first cause, unmoved mover, or the like, but no longer directly involved in and at work in it. This view was given classical expression during the late seventeenth and eighteenth centuries under the name deism. Another, associated with philosophers like the Dutch Jew Spinoza, has been pantheism, in which God and the world are seen as being practically identical—although Spinoza himself was prepared to talk about differing modes of God as nature. A third conception is known as theism, in which God is taken to be both transcendent to the world but also present in it. Theism would appear to take a middle path between talk of God's remoteness in deism and talk of God's identification with the world in pantheism. But there are theisms and theisms—not a single and generally accepted view, but a variety of ways of speaking of God as "above" yet with or in the creation.

As we all know, there are those who deny God altogether. The atheist thinks that talk about a supreme reality, a worshipful reality, a suprahuman reality, is nonsense. For him, if he is consistent in his beliefs, the only genuine existent is the world which we know and in which we live; there is nothing whatever beyond, above, or behind it. Hence the consistent atheist is in fact a positivist who would confine attention to the world of human experience or observation and reject the claims of believers in God as absurd or undemonstrable or wishful thinking. Probably there are very few entirely consistent atheists today. However, there are many who would say they are agnostic about God, his existence, his nature, his purpose, and his activity. There *may* be a divine reality; if so, we know nothing about it and it is wiser to attend to matters of human concern—after all, "the proper study of mankind" is man himself, they would say, and it is unnecessary to concern ourselves with anything else. At their best, such men and women are "humanists," not in the sense that word was given in the high Renaissance but in a modern meaning, which is the centering of interest and concern on human life, human welfare, and human possibilities. In reaction against the pretentious claims, as they would say, made in the past by many theologians, they think that such a human-centered point of view is healthier, wiser, and more likely to be beneficial. But if there is a God, he is remote or "deistic."

We are also aware of some people who are quite prepared to speak of "the inner God," the depths of the human spirit which are not to be reduced to mere phenomenal experiences but which speak out of and speak to some spiritual reality which may not be transcendent to man and which need not entail talk about a God who is other than man, but which is yet to be reckoned with as given in human experience at its finest and most exalted. Such people are often enough ready to use language which sounds pantheistic, but for the most part they do not wish to make any metaphysical or ontological statements about what they are sure is present in man. For them, religious language is at best mythological or symbolic; it is a way of pointing to this inner experience, although it has no reference to anything beyond that experience. The kind of mythology or symbol of which they are talking is human, but human at its best; it is not myth or symbol whose significance is in expressing something that is beyond and other than human by language of a metaphorical or poetical or imaginative sort.

If for the moment we exclude traditional theism from our discussion, to return to a possible revision of it later in this chapter and again in the next and last chapter, we are confronted with deism, with humanism, and with what might well be styled subjectivism or spiritism. Pantheism is also to be excluded from our present consideration, since it is not usually found among ordinary people but largely confined to sophisticated thinkers—although we must grant that in a certain sense there is a pantheistic element in the thought of many who would speak about deity in nature and yet would not have any clear ideas about exactly what this meant. The best expression of such a pantheistic touch in ordinary people's thought could very well be the odd hymn included in the volume *Songs of Praise*, with its words: "God comes down in the rain and the crop grows tall;   This is the country faith, and best of all."

We shall now look at deism, humanism, and subjectivism or spiritism, and we shall attempt to see what values each of these may maintain as well as what dangers may be present in each. But first it may be noticed that each has a certain relationship to one of the modes of being and activity which Christian triunitarianism asserts. Thus deism has a certain correspondence with the transcendence of God as creative source and origin. Humanism calls to mind the concomitance of God alongside and with his creatures. Subjectivism or spiritism has its resemblance to God as immanent, enabling the response of the human mind, heart, and spirit to the divine reality expressed in the creation. As we proceed we shall see how each has meaning and attempts to say something important about aspects of human experience or observation of the world. The difficulty in each of them is that it may become so dominant that a rounded and adequate picture of God, the world, and humankind is made impossible.

Deism, as we have said, was given its classical expression in the late seventeenth and eighteenth century in England, and to some degree on the continent as well; Voltaire is an excellent example of a thinker who had deistic views. It was an appropriate theological position in an age when a mechanical model of the creation had become popular among intellectuals. After all, the world seemed to run on the lines of a machine which had been brought into existence in the distant past and which now appeared to run according to laws "which never shall be broken" but which God had ordained in the very act of creation. God was an absentee God, who did not intrude into the orderly progression of nature; or, if he did, it was only by miracles required to correct some defect in nature's operation or possibly to reveal something of himself not manifest in any of the observed regularities.

Inevitably, such a view made God irrelevant in the ordinary experience of men and women, save insofar as he had set up moral laws which, like the "laws of nature," must be obeyed. His requirements were that his human creatures should live "a sober, righteous, and godly life." Mystical experience, religious experience, and enthusiasm in religious life were looked upon with suspicion. To all intents and purposes, God did not count for much in the day-by-day existence of men and women. He was the necessary first cause of whatever the world might contain and do, but there was little if any immediate awareness of him or experience of him.

Now the value in such a deistic position is to be found in one and only one point: this is that deism was a way in which the divine transcendence was asserted, although that assertion was made in a manner which was mistaken and misleading. Properly interpreted, transcendence has nothing to do with spatial and certainly not with a temporal remoteness from the creation. As the theologians of the Middle Ages well understood, the essential meaning of belief in divine transcendence is its teaching us that God is not exhausted, or completely "used up" (as we might say), by what happens in the world. There is the "more" in God which renders him utterly *inexhaustible*; there are reserves of energy and of love which no creature can comprehend and which no activity of God can entirely encompass. The truth in deism is not in its crude picture of an artificer who once made a world and then let it operate by its own internal laws; rather, its truth is in its recognition, however wrong the manner in which that is indicated, that there is more in God than the creation can ever contain or express.

The humanist emphasis so often found today also has its value. The truth that each of us is indeed "a man for others"—to employ the phrase which Bonhoeffer used in speaking of Jesus—is very important and needs continual emphasis. Tertullian once wrote that "when you see your brother, you see your Lord." In a theistic perspective this tells us something about God's concomitance, his incarnational presence and action in the world. But without that theistic context, humanism can be valuable in its own right, if it leads men and women to devote themselves to the well-being of their fellows and to do all in their power to secure true happiness for others by way of social justice, sympathy, and assistance. The contemptuous dismissal of this sort of humanism, so frequently expressed by religious people, is misguided and unfair. On the other hand, too great a stress upon the humanistic approach—indeed, an exclusive concern for the divine concomitance within a theistic context—can lead to a practical atheism, just as much as can a deistic conception of God himself. Instead of Tertullian's profound teaching that in seeing our brother we see something of *God*, what can result will be the tautological assertion that in seeing, and serving, our brother or sister we have entirely exhausted the truth about that human being—we know him or her as a fellow human and that is all there is to the matter.

To put this in christological language, when we say that Jesus is "the man for others" we have not adequately explained or even envisaged the full reality of Jesus. First of all he was "the man for God," and unless Christian insight be utterly erroneous he was also, in some deep way, the man whom God sent, in whom God worked, and in seeing and serving whom we are seeing and serving God. Thus there is both a value in humanism and a danger that it may be content to remain in a partial and inadequate view of human nature.

When we turn to the third of our possible views, subjectivism or spiritism, we discover that much the same is also the case. There is great value in emphasizing the reality and importance of subjective experience; there is an equal value in stressing the place of the spirit in humankind which is more than, and is quite unexhausted by, our ordinary run of experience, our day-by-day ventures, our modes of behavior, and the like. Any interpretation of human nature which fails to grasp the depths in our existence, the utter importance of our subjective apprehension, and the reality of the inner life which makes us different from "the beasts that perish," is convicted of reducing us to a sub-human level. But unless this human subjectivity is also seen in its relationship to that which is around human existence, and beyond and above that existence, it does not do full justice to the depths which each man or woman knows in himself or herself. Thus subjectivism or spiritism can be seen to have its own contribution to make, but it can also be seen that taken alone it can lead, like deism or humanism, to practical atheism.

What we need is a balanced view, in which the values of each of these—deism, humanism, and subjectivism—will be preserved, but in which each will be put in its proper relation to the other two. The result will be a proportionate understanding, taking account of all the facts and yet in each case corrected and complemented by emphases which also need to be accepted and given due recognition.

When we look around us today we can see that these three views are by no means unknown; in fact, most people accept one or another of the three, unless they are unwilling to make any assumptions about, or engage in any statements concerning, the reality which they know and experience. There is a good deal of deism in contemporary thought, although that word may not be used. Many men and women are quite ready to say that they believe the world does not explain itself and hence that there must have been some source or origin which will account for its existence. But they are not prepared to go much beyond that, save to insist that we ought to live a decent life as good citizens, with a certain concern for justice and even for benevolence. They are witnessing in their own way to the truth which was contained in the old cosmological argument for God; they may also be said to witness to the fact that whatever is said about the divine must be set in the context of mystery. But their position, taken in itself, has no genuine bearing upon their daily lives; they live as if God were not.

Again, there are vast numbers of people deeply concerned for their fellow humans. These are the men and women who support movements for world peace and understanding, for social justice, for understanding in human relations, and much else that is both good and right. So far as they can see, however, this is all that is required of them; they are content to rest in a purely this-worldly attitude and might well be astonished if they were told that apart from something more deeply present in human existence there is no particular reason for their valiant struggle on behalf of their fellows. They have got hold of an important, indeed an absolutely necessary, point or aspect in human affairs; but they have no grounding for their admirable desire to help others—and what is more, they are all too easily discouraged when there is little if any response to their strenuous efforts to improve the human lot.

The same may be said of subjectivism or spiritism. The cultivation of the inner life, through whatever disciplines and techniques may be available, is invaluable. A man or woman who lives entirely on the surface of things is likely to be a pretty poor specimen of humankind. Those who seek to develop their life through openness to beauty, for example, are admirable people. But can it be said that the cultivation of one's own inner life will ultimately satisfy our deepest needs and desires, unless in some fashion that inner life is in touch with how things go in the world at large and can be related to a reality that is beyond and above the subjectivity which is admittedly so important? I think that the answer to this question is a plain no. This is demonstrated by the sense of impoverishment, the feeling of futility, the loss of nerve, and the readiness to give up the inner disciplines, which we so frequently observe in those who strenuously insist on, and equally strenuously have sought to develop, their human spirit in its finer and more exacting characteristics. Men and women who are *only* concerned for the growth of their subjective selves can often be practical atheists; they can also become despairing and disappointed human beings.

So I should wish to contend that in pointing toward the transcendence or inexhaustibility of "whatever is divine," deism has had something important to say. Likewise I should wish to contend that in emphasizing the service of one's fellows, humanism can teach us that each of us is "his brother's keeper" and that we have a responsibility for the welfare of that brother. And I should wish to contend, finally, that the development of the human spirit in its subjective reality is to be welcomed as much better than the centering of attention on material goods in the vulgar sense, since human existence is never likely to be satisfied by the accumulation of possessions and the provision of adequate means of making a livelihood.

On the other hand, I should wish to contend that the right balance can be achieved only when the transcendent, the inexhaustible and mysterious reality by which we are surrounded and which constitutes our final environment, is perceived to be most intimately related to the demands of our human situation, so that the service of our fellows is in the long run nothing other than a service done to that divine reality. I should wish also to contend that until and unless the deep subjectivity of the human race, the innermost spirit, is somehow seen to be related to the circumambient reality who can be apprehended, to some extent at least, in other human beings with whom we live and for whom we are prepared to give ourselves, such subjectivity, however highly cultivated, is lacking in abiding significance and can be the pursuit of what is only an illusion.

Or to put it in theological language, only when God as transcendent, God as concomitant, and God as immanent are accepted as present in, active through, self-identified with, concerned for, and known by men and women can we make real sense of human existence. Only in this way can we be delivered from practical atheism and opened to the possibility of a life which is rich and full precisely because it is in touch with God our heavenly Parent through each of the three modes of activity in the creation.

Suppose it is granted that we need a doctrine of God which will preserve the values in deism, humanism, and spiritism; which will hold these in balance; and which will not in the end succumb either to the "absenteeism" of an entirely deistic conception or to the identification of God and creation which might follow from too unrestrained an acceptance of humanism or spiritism and which would be in fact nothing other than pantheism. In my view the proper position would best be described by the not frequently used term panentheism. Notice that we are speaking of pan-*en*-theism, which might be translated as "everything has its existence *in* God but yet is not to be taken as *identical with* God." Or we might say that this is a position which sees God *in* everything—in that case, perhaps, "theo-en-panism" might be the appropriate, if barbarous, term to distinguish the position from "theopanism," a term sometimes used to describe Spinoza's teaching, which spoke of *deus sive natura*—God identical with nature, although in different degrees of identity. In any event, the panentheistic conception can rightly be said to be the only variety of theistic philosophy which guarantees the values in deism, humanism, and spiritism while at the same time so ordering those values that there is a sound balance in what is said of deity.

The word itself was first used by the German philosopher K. C. F. Krause (who lived from 1781 to 1832). Krause devised a theistic philosophy which taught that

God's "being" as well as his "act" includes within it the whole creation, but he insisted that this existence of all things "in God" did not in any sense deny a genuine transcendence of God, since God was more than—and completely free to act in—the creation; his argument was that if we take seriously the involvement of deity in a creation which matters seriously to him, that creation must in some sense "exist in him." Some have suggested that the earlier French theistic philosopher Nicolas Malebranche, who wrote in the late sixteenth and early seventeenth centuries, anticipated Krause's view; but this is not entirely certain, although his thought did stress the notion that the whole creation was so set up, as it were, that a specific incarnation at a given point, in Jesus, was both prepared for and in some degree given anticipatory expression. To speak in that way, of course, is to approach the incarnational or sacramental interpretation of the cosmos for which I have already argued in earlier chapters of this book.

The great Anglo- or Scottish-German philosophical theologian Friedrich von Hügel, who died in 1925, accepted and used the word panentheism in his effort to preserve both the transcendence of God and the divine action in and through all nature and history. But it has been Prof. Charles Hartshorne, the living American philosopher of religion and the leading exponent in philosophical circles of Process Thought, who has most consistently spoken of the panentheistic world-view. It is he also who has suggested the relation of the soul or mind to the body as a better analogy than the more conventional ruler-ruled, monarch-subject, or even creator-creation one. Interestingly, Prof. John Macquarrie, who is by no means a wholehearted disciple of Whitehead or Hartshorne, has been ready to use the same analogy. His inaugural lecture as Lady Margaret Professor at Oxford and his recent book *Thinking About God* (London: SCM Press, 1975) both contain several favorable references to the analogy as providing an alternative, although not a substitute, for the more usual analogies which are monarchical in character.

We may find a use of that same analogy in Thomas Aquinas, although this has not often been noticed. In one place in Aquinas we read, "In his rule God stands in relation to the whole universe as the soul stands in relation to the body" (*II Sent.* dist. 1, q.1, ad 1). Here, in the philosophical theologian who is regarded by the Roman Catholic Church as the exponent of the strictest orthodoxy, we find an approach which if taken seriously illuminates a good deal else in the corpus of Aquinas' writings; it may even lend some slight weight to the charge made now and again that Aquinas has a tendency toward a quasi-pantheistic view of God and the world. That, of course, is absurd. But it may very well be the case that the Angelic Doctor would have been glad to accept a general panentheistic world-view had he possessed the terminology which would make it possible and had he been able to free himself from the Aristotelian notion of "unmoved mover" and Greek-derived notions of "primal substance" in talk about God.

However this may be, it is my contention that the only variety of theism which will serve us is indeed a panentheistic one, while the analogy of soul-body or mind-body will prove most helpful in our interpretation of how God and the creation are related. Above all, this kind of theism will deliver us from the apparently almost inescapable tendency of ordinary theism to end up in what is really deism, with God so separated from his world that in the end of the day it seems to be irrelevant to him and can in no way affect or influence him. To speak of God and world in *that* fashion is certainly to do serious damage to the consistent biblical portrayal of God's self-identification with his creation, on the one hand, and to the deliverance of religious life that God takes into account the creation and its achievements and failures, on the other. What is more, only in a panentheistic context can we satisfactorily find a way for the retaining of the inherited triunitarian picture of God—or so I am convinced.

To some it may seem that the soul-body or mind-body analogy is very dangerous. Will it not bring us to a quasi-pantheistic position despite all that has been said? My answer would be that it will depend upon how we envisage the relationship of soul or mind and body. If we have a social conception of human nature, an "organismic" view, to use Whitehead's not very happy word, we shall see that we ourselves are complex creatures in whom mind (or soul) and body are not identical but are distinct yet closely knit together. Our mind is the chief directive agency in our existence; to it our body responds. At the same time, what goes on in the body influences and affects the mind. This is a familiar theme nowadays, with the widespread knowledge of psychosomatics in medicine and elsewhere. There is a profound sense in which the mind is distinct from but yet includes the body and exists in the body, but this without negating the facticity of the body and its genuine "independence" of the mind. Above all, the analogy is useful because it puts the emphasis on the persuasive rather than compulsive or coercive nature of the fashion in which the mind, with its aims, its thought, its awareness of lures and attractions, works upon (and hence influences and affects) bodily functioning. One might almost speak of a "gracious" character in this working.

But if it stands alone, without the addition of the diverse ways in which mind works with, upon, and in the body, the analogy would not be satisfactory. On the other hand, with that perfectly proper and valid addition, it becomes most helpful to us. Obviously, there is no possibility of a precise correspondence between those diverse ways of mind's activity in respect to the body and God's ways of working in the creation. Every analogy will fail at some point and in any event should never be pressed so far that it amounts almost to literal predication; when that happens, it is no longer analogy. I am sure, however, that this manner of thinking about God and his creation, with whatever difficulties it may contain, is more suitable for our purpose than the more conventional use of the models drawn from imperial courts with God as a dictatorial ruler and the world with its human creatures as subjects whose duty is to cringe before him in abject submission. Professor Macquarrie has made this point admirably in the recent book already mentioned, and I need not dwell upon it. All I need remark here is that a triunitarian understanding of God's modes of being and activity—and always remembering that God's being *is* his activity, as Karl Barth has said—when combined with the analogy I have proposed gives us a view of the divine and worshipful reality which is in accordance with the great Johannine text that God is Love and that he must never be conceived as primarily coercive will.

In concluding this chapter I wish to make some quotations from an interesting essay lately written by the Czech theologian J. M. Lochman and published in the journal *Theology* (1975, vol. LXXVII, pp. 173–83). Although there is a strongly Barthian flavor about what he says, at point after point this distinguished contemporary makes the same insistence that has been present in this book. For example, "The triune God is *the* Christian concept of God." And again, the following splendid summary:

In its trinitarian concept of God Christian faith is referring to the "relational" God, God in relation. God is no "relationless God," "God relates"—and indeed not only to the world outside, but also within himself. He relates within himself in relationships which are called by name, and hence are personally structured. Of course this fundamental relational character of God was manifested to early Christian thinkers primarily in the experiences which they had themselves with God, specifically in the Christ event. . . . The God of this revelation is the God who relates. His personal activity is not merely an "accident" but his revealed "essence." He cannot be conceived in impersonal, relationless terms. Hence the early Church Fathers struggled through to the trinitarian concept of God. Their doctrine of the "immanent Trinity," even though it gives the appearance of being speculative, is in no way merely speculative, but rather reflects the personal-existential concern of their faith.

Lochman is especially interesting in using the contribution of the German theologian Erik

Peterson in his untranslated book *Monotheism as a Political Problem* to show that the older monotheistic tradition "which involved viewing God in the form of an imperial ruler" is "a highly questionable reinterpretation of the biblical understanding of God." It was "in this context that the trinitarian concept of God took on an important and liberating role," since it "shattered the idea of the divine monarchy" and thus made possible a due recognition of the social relationships in which God stands to his world. Here, of course, is the point which we have been making in talking of a panentheistic view with a social-personal analogy for God, coupled with the use of the soul-body analogy for the mode of relationship between God and world.

The Czech writer goes on to stress the manner in which the doctrine of the triune God has brought to us a new awareness of the compassion of God, which denies the old idea that God is "apathetic" or without participation in the world's suffering as well as the world's joy. He goes to the length of saying that "God is no being divorced from suffering, no apathetic being. God's being is in suffering. In this way a true 'revolution in the concept of God' occurs in trinitarian thinking." And he concludes with these words:

These three dimensions [God's three modes] which have included the personal, social, and compassionate character of the triune God, may be thought of as . . . converging lines. If I had ultimately and comprehensively to describe their point of convergence in one word, I would risk saying that God's being is in love. . . . The personal, social, and compassionate character of God is expressed in this one word in a concrete and comprehensive way.

Lochman's essay is concerned to emphasize what he styles "the lasting relevance of the doctrine of the Trinity for human life." I can only hope that in this book that same point has been made with sufficient clarity. And I should wish to echo Lochman's further insistence that there are enormous implications in the triunitarian conception of God for every aspect of human existence, including the political and ethical ones to which he gives special attention. But to dwell upon this would be to write another book, and our concern here is much more with the philosophical and theological importance and value of the doctrine.

In the issue of *Theology* in which Lochman's essay makes its appearance, Dr. David Braine writes an extended "response" to what Lochman has to say. He closes that response (p. 190) with some words which I should like to make my own and with which I end this chapter:

The doctrine of the Trinity transforms, not in a merely speculative but in an historically-rooted and kerygmatically driven way, the dry bones of the otherwise merely logical or metaphysical conception that, in God, to be, to live, and to love are the same, and does this in a way which at the same time exhibits him as communicating this love to us.

6
An
Effort at
Reconception

In the preceding chapters of this book we have looked at the primitive Christian experience as this is reflected in the pages of the books of the New Testament. We have seen how that threefold experience became the basic material for the formulation of a doctrine of the triunity of God, a task undertaken during the first four centuries of the Christian tradition and achieved with the use, inevitably and naturally, of such philosophical presuppositions as were entertained by the Fathers who engaged in the task. We have gone on to see the way in which some such threefold interpretation of the one God's nature and activity fits in with and gives deeper meaning to the continuing Christian life with God in Christ through the Spirit; and, beyond that, we have recognized that the same three-in-one way of approach is of value in speaking to us of God as God over us, God with us, and God in us. What is more, we have tried to show how this leads us to a deeper understanding of the significance of talk about God as creator, God as revealer, and God as inspirer. Finally, we have sought to indicate that some such model helps enormously in bringing together the insights found in each of the three types of religious teaching which in one way or another, at one place or another, and at one time or another, have been influential: the deistic line, the humanist line, and the subjective-experiential line. None of these is satisfactory if taken alone; when brought together, and finding a place in a wider conception, their several insights and the sort of religious life they engender can be given focus and point.

God is indeed transcendent, but he is also immanent. These two do not exhaust the divine reality, for God is also concomitant—alongside and with his creation as well as more than and unexhausted by creation, and also most intimately working "from below" (as it were) to conform creation to his intention and to enable it, without denial of creaturely freedom, to respond to him and hence realize its fullest potentiality.

Our task in this chapter is to seek after some fashion in which the abiding reality of the triunitarian religious life, and the insight which this provides into "how things really go in the world," may be stated which will be relevant to our own time and place. Like our ancestors in the faith, we must have some conceptuality which will be appropriate for us because it speaks meaningfully to us about the world as we know it, experience it, and seek to interpret it—quite apart from the specific deliverances of the Christian faith which we profess. As I have urged, every generation must proceed in this manner; ours is no exception.

In other books, and in articles in various journals, I have argued that the best available conceptuality for this enterprise of reconception is Process Thought. In North America and Australia, more recently in Britain and on the continent, this conceptuality has become a matter of interest to philosophers and (in North America particularly) also to theologians. Process Thought gets its name from the Gifford lectures of Alfred North Whitehead, which were given in 1927–28 at Edinburgh and published immediately afterward by the Cambridge University Press in Britain and Macmillan in New York; their title was *Process and Reality*. I shall not attempt here a sketch of Process Thought in any detail. Several books are readily available which do this, some of which are intended for the general reader: *The Creative Advance* by E. H. Peters (St. Louis, Mo.: Bethany Press, 1966); *The Living God and the Modern World* by P. N. Hamilton (London: Hodder and Stoughton, 1967; Philadelphia: United

Church Press, 1967); *Man's Vision of God* by Charles Hartshorne (New York: Harper & Brothers, 1941); and two volumes of my own, *Process Thought and Christian Faith* (Digswell Place, Welwyn: Nisbet, 1968) and *Alfred North Whitehead* (London: Lutterworth Press, 1969). It will serve our present purpose if I set down here, briefly enough, the main emphases in this conceptuality and then attempt to apply them to the discussion of the doctrine of God as triune.

Whitehead in the first place and, after him, Charles Hartshorne (who was Whitehead's assistant at Harvard University during the early days of his professorship in the American Cambridge after his many years at the English one) have sought to work out a view of the world which takes account of our evolutionary perspective and which goes beyond the metaphysical systems that were dominant in the late nineteenth and early twentieth century, whether these were "naturalistic" or "idealist." Hence the initial emphasis to which we must call attention is the stress upon the "processive" or evolutionary nature of the world. With this is associated the conviction that this world is not composed of things or substantial entities but rather of events or occurrences. The ultimate constituents are focusings of energy, which in various configurations present us with the material of our experience. Modern physics is familiar enough with this idea, having replaced the notion of hard and infrangible things by that of energetic charges which arrange themselves in such patterns that we may speak of atoms, molecules, etc., but which are very different from the older conception of "stuff" of which the universe was thought to be made up. These "energy-events," to use Prof. John Hick's phrase, are called by Whitehead "actual entities," a somewhat unhappy definition, to be sure, since it may suggest the very "thing" idea which he wished to avoid.

Not only do we have to do with a world that is in movement or process, composed of charges of energy (or events or happenings) which are experienced; that world is also marked by a social quality in which everything affects and influences everything else. The past perishes in one sense, but its consequences are not lost since each given moment in that past has its place in what follows after. The name given in Process Thought to this influence or affect is "prehension," in that every occasion grasps or feels that which makes its impact upon it. Here, once again, modern physical science provides evidence for this interpretation. But in our own human experience we are equally participant in a processive movement, linking the momentary experiences which are ours and requiring from us decisions among possibilities that the past has both presented to us and made relevant for us.

I have just used the word decision, and this points us to yet another characteristic of our world. At the human level we make decisions in a more or less fully conscious fashion, choosing among possibilities that the past has offered us, in the light of present demands and lures, and toward a future realization in which we may find what we think to be our proper satisfaction or fulfillment. At other levels in the world, however, there is also something analogous to such decision. Obviously it is not present in the conscious sense known to us; yet if we recognize that the word decision is derived from the Latin word for "cutting off," we can see that when (to take a simple example) a quantum of energy makes its "jump" in one direction, it is "cutting off" (hence, deciding against) other possible directions. In this sense there is an unpredictability about the world. This is not *sheer* "chanciness," if I may coin the word, but an indeterminacy within the broad limits set by what is a *cosmos*, a world of pattern and order, and not anarchy or chaos. The world is one where freedom is a fact of experience and observation, although when we look back we seem to see a determinate movement. To deny the freedom which we experience and see, and to stress only the subsequent appearance of determination, is to entertain a theory that (as C. D. Broad put it) is "so silly that only a very learned person could have thought it up."

I have stressed process, but I have not identified this with *progress*. The latter term would suggest that there is an almost inevitable improvement—that "day by day, in every way, things are getting better and better," as they used to say in the halcyon period of liberal thought. There may be such an improvement, but there may also be movement which produces a worse situation. Each of us may choose that which will fulfill us; we may also choose what will do anything but fulfill us. In the world there are backwaters, deviations, a retarding of advance. This is apparent at many levels; in the realm of human experience, it shows itself not only in suffering, pain, disease, and the like but also (and tragically) in the sphere of moral decision where, by self-centered and narrow concern for our own aggrandizement at the cost of others, we can and do impede the movement toward good and genuinely fulfilling ends.

Finally, Process thought places much stress on the enormous strength of persuasion in a world that sometimes appears to be largely a matter of sheer and senseless coercion or force. Whitehead urged that the history of humankind is the story of the way in which the wisest came slowly to recognize the priority of persuasion over force. It takes a long time for others to accept this point of view, yet we discover in all cultures and civilizations an awareness of it and at least a verbal assent to it. But with this kind of increasing awareness of persuasion's priority, there is also the possibility of tragic choices against persuasion; for "the higher we may rise, the farther we may fall." Persuasion—which may also be called love—is always a possibility, but it can be denied, rejected, or made into an occasion for subtle control which is really nothing other than coercion in disguise.

While not all who accept Process Thought are theists, the many who do hold a theistic position agree with Whitehead in affirming that God cannot be "an exception" to whatever principles have been found necessary to account for and explain the way things go more generally; rather, God must be "the chief exemplification" of such principles. If this be the case—and the argument for it is along lines of consistency and coherence in thought—then God is the dynamic, living, event-full, related, free reality who is not the only but who is the *chief* causative principle. Furthermore, God must be the chief recipient from the creation, who accepts and uses what that creation accomplishes. He works upon the world primarily through the lure and attraction which he exerts. The divine use of coercion is only in the establishment of the limits which prevent cosmos from turning into chaos, patterning from becoming anarchy. There is a point beyond which the creation's freedom cannot go without itself becoming self-destructive. Finally, God is both "primordial," in that he provides the possibilities among which choice is made, and "consequent," in that he is recipient of the consequences of creaturely decision. Above all, he is all-wise love who uses for his purpose of further creative advance all that is accomplished or achieved—save for the "surd" of evil which *as evil* he cannot accept but which can be absorbed so that it may become an occasion for a good that might not otherwise be available. But how can such a conception of God be related to the God about whom the Jewish and Christian scriptures speak and to whose activity in the world they bear witness?

Briefly—and I have no time here to develop this theme in the fullness which it merits—the model of God which is presented in this theistic version of Process Thought is very close to the biblical picture. In the Bible God is the living and active one, who is at work in his world and affected by that world. There is joy in God at the world's good and sorrow at the world's wrong; there is an adaptation of God's action to the situations in which humans find themselves; there is a loving care which never lets go and which labors unfailingly for the fulfillment of his children. His principal mode of working is through the worship he inspires (as Whitehead liked to say), the lure which he offers, and the sheer attraction of his positive goodness in action.

The biblical story begins as I urged earlier, with a response made by a primitive people to manifestations of power in unnatural events such as earthquake, volcanic eruption, and storm. In the desert days of the ancient Jewish tribes it was this which captured their reverence and awakened their awed response. But as time went on, men like Moses began to grasp something much more profound. The power which was released in the world of natural events was a "power that makes for righteousness," to use again Matthew Arnold's well-known phrase. Righteousness like that was on the side of those who would respond faithfully to the purposes of God; furthermore, that same righteousness expected from men and women a corresponding justice in their dealings one with another. The years passed; the Jews entered the "promised land" of Canaan; and in that land, under the guidance of a series of great prophets, people of unusual insight and understanding who also were making their response to what was happening among them and to them and in them, there was disclosed a deeper truth: namely, that the God whom they worshiped was primarily marked by the quality which they knew as loving-kindness, mercy, faithful care. Thus it was that the highest point in the development of Jewish religion was reached when the fatherly care of God was stressed; he was the one who welcomed and accepted everyone, of whatever nation, who turned to him.

Jesus appeared, his way prepared by what had gone before him because he was a Jew who believed the religion which his forefathers had come to accept as the truth. In his words and in his actions he expressed outwardly his conviction, born doubtless from his own inner experience, that the God of Israel, who was also God of all the world, would not only receive and welcome and accept any who turned to him but he would also, and this is the central point, go out to seek and find his children and lure them to himself by his love. As we urged in the opening chapter of this book, the first Christians believed, with all their hearts, that this same love—this Lover, for it is God himself—was given human statement in the total event of Jesus Christ, living among men and women in his days in Palestine and after his crucifixion still living among them as the risen Lord. They were impelled to respond, and the New

Testament is the record of the many different ways in which that response was given. It was a response of enormous power but utterly personalizing in its character; it was so all-compelling in its persuasive strength that those first Christians could only interpret it, as we have seen, in terms of what they had read in the Jewish scriptures about the Spirit who was to be poured out from God on all people. Thus as these first believers, and during the succeeding centuries millions of other believers, "prehended" (to use now the technical Process Thought language) God's working upon them in outgoing and inviting love and on their own part were prehended by that very same Love in action, they came to speak in the threefold idiom to which we have so constantly made reference.

In other words, there is a kind of fit between the reality of the Christian experience and the facts to which this points, on the one hand, and the insight and teaching of Process Thought, on the other. Nor is this fit accidental. On the contrary, it has come about because whether they wish it or not Process Thought's theistic exponents are bound to take into account the tradition which they inherit, the continuing experience which that tradition conveys, and the intuition which it offers as to how things go in the world and how things go in God, as he is in himself because he is as he acts in the world.

With the situation which we have outlined so far in this chapter, we are now prepared to go on in our attempt to see how the triunitarian model for God, received from our long inheritance of life in faith, can be worked out in terms of that conceptuality which seems so appropriate and meaningful in our own day. And here we need to remember that nobody is claiming, least of all those who, like me, subscribe to the Process conceptuality, that we have arrived at the final truth about everything. The Process way of seeing the world may be, and I believe that it is, the best way available to us today; but it has in its very nature an inbuilt protection against absurd claims to finality. On the other hand, we need to remember that the fundamental affirmations of Christian faith stand secure, in that they are built upon facts of experience, but the specific theological construction which seeks to give them coherence and consistency is not the "last word." What abides is the reality of the supremely worshipful reality we call God; the revelatory activity of God in history and nature and in human experience, brought to its focus in Jesus Christ; and the impulse of response in commitment and discipleship, in a fellowship of trusting men and women, about which we speak when we talk of the Holy Spirit.

In his second series of Lowell lectures, published in 1960 under the title *Religion in the Making* in a Living Age paperback, Whitehead wrote these words: "Christ gave his life. It is for Christians to discern the doctrine" (p. 55). He contrasted Christ with Buddha in this respect, pointing out that the latter had been concerned to set forth what Whitehead called "a metaphysic"—perhaps we should rather say a philosophy. The significant point here is that the process of development which we have traced earlier in this book is essentially a "discerning" of doctrine.

Primarily this was the doctrine of the person and work of Christ himself, teaching that in him God had "visited and redeemed his people" and working out the position which later became the dogma of the Incarnation. This tells us, in formal terms, that in Jesus Christ—in the total event which we indicate when we speak his name, including preparation for him, his own life and doings, his crucifixion and death, and what followed after when his presence and power were once again known and a response was made to him in faith and discipleship—God has acted in a signal manner. Here is a genuine human existence in every respect like our own, save that in it there was a full obedience to God's purpose (hence Jesus was said, in the idiom of the time, to be "without sin"); but here also is an activity of God carried out in and through that human existence. God who is the cosmic Lover has expressed himself decisively in the human loving which was and is Jesus.

But the "discerning" of doctrine went beyond this; as we have shown, it took the form of a portrayal of God in himself and in his activity in the world as "three-in-one"—the triunitarian model for God. This development was based upon experienced facts, whose implications were grasped and whose significance was given statement by talk of God the Father, God the Word or Son, and God the Holy Spirit, who yet must be affirmed as *one* God.

In that same book, *Religion in the Making*, Whitehead says something else: "Religion claims that its concepts, though derived primarily from special experiences, are yet of universal validity, to be applied by faith to the ordering of all experience" (p. 31); and he goes on to affirm that "rational religion appeals to the direct intuition of special occasions, and to the elucidatory power of its concepts for all occasions." This is why he can urge that "the doctrines of rational religion aim at being that metaphysics which can be derived from the supernormal experience of mankind in its moments of finest insight" (*ibid.*), so that a wider generality may be claimed for that which is made known in the specific instances in which men and women have experienced, as they would assert, the working of God in and upon their lives.

I should not wish to argue that the doctrine of the Godhead as triune is to be found given within the conceptuality of Process Thought. Nor do I think that it is possible to take the triunitarian view of deity as nothing other than a restatement of the categories of Whiteheadian, Hartshorne-ian, or any other variety of Process Thought. This is why I find it difficult to accept Professor Cobb's comment, in the review already cited, that the "distinction" between "God as operative alongside of and upon nature, history, and human lives *and* God as operative within and through these," to quote my own words from *The Holy Spirit* (Philadelphia: United Church Press, 1974, p. 40), makes little sense in the Whiteheadian conceptuality which I accept.

Naturally, I should have thought, this distinction is not to be found, as such, within that conceptuality.

On the other hand, it may be the case (and I believe that it *is* the case) that the deliverance of Christian existence, with its obvious presentation of just that distinction which I sought to indicate and which in this book has been examined from many different angles, may "fit into," even if it is not exactly present in, the Process conceptuality. In any event, Whitehead's own position would indicate that our primary appeal is to those "special experiences" (in this case the data of Christian life in faith) which are then used in an effort to make more general their meaning and hence to "apply them by faith to the ordering of all experience." And there can be no doubt, it seems to me, that these "special experiences" which are the basis for Christian understanding do in fact give us precisely the distinction between the operation of God "upon nature, history, and human lives" and the operation of God "within and through these."

We have seen that in the scriptural use of terms there is no clear and precise way in which this distinction is made. To put it simply, "Word" and "Spirit" are often used as if they pointed at the same reality. Yet at the same time, and despite this confusion of language, there can be a genuine distinction which is more profound and important than terminological considerations. God *is* represented as working toward and with his creation; God *is* seen also as working within and through the conditions of creaturely existence. In the former, God is disclosed through what takes place in the world of nature, in the events of history, and as he speaks to men and women; in the latter, God is disclosed as enabling a response to be made to these revelatory data in nature, history, and human life.

Professor Cobb has suggested that within the Whiteheadian conceptuality we may properly speak of the Spirit "as the divine work which heightens and perfects the universal work of God as the principle of life" (this quotation is again from Professor Cobb's stimulating review, to which I have already referred). He goes on to say that this "divine work" of heightening and perfecting "might be associated with 'the particular providence for particular occasions' which is 'the love of God for the world' " (the quotation by Cobb is from Whitehead's *Process and Reality*, p. 532).

I am quite prepared to accept this notion, provided that it does not lead us into two mistakes. The first of these would be to *confine* the working of God *as Word* to Jesus Christ as known to the Christian community and to it alone. To do this would be to deny that pervasive self-revelation of God upon which the mainstream of our tradition has always insisted. It would be to narrow the "universal applicability" of the special Christian experience and remove it from the wider context which the fathers of the church were so intent upon preserving. It would be "falsely christocentric," in von Hügel's phrase, for it would be to deny that the Word of God "is the light that lightens every man" and the agency which is indeed "the principle of *all* life," to put it in Cobb's own wording, but with the emphasis added. The second mistake would be to think that "the love of God for the world" is *exclusively* recognized in this or that "particular providence for particular occasions," rather than to see that love in *all* divine operations. God's love for the world is manifested in the very creativity which belongs properly to him; it is disclosed in the working out of "the principle of life," whenever and wherever this is present—and that is everywhere. It may be *distinctively* revealed in those "particular providences"; above all, it may be (and we have argued that it is) known most intimately and deeply in the "heightening and perfecting" which characterizes the response made to what God accomplishes in the event of Jesus Christ and in the Christian fellowship as it is caught up into and made participant in that response. But I should contend that it is also and always a matter of "universal validity," as Whitehead put it; and I should also contend that this wider and more inclusive position provides material for a theology which goes beyond and yet does not contradict the Whiteheadian, or any other Process, conceptuality.

God in his concrete actuality as related to the creation is God as we have to do with him in real experience. God as "primordial," providing the continuum of possibility in the world, is abstract; this is simply God as *existing*, rather than God in his full and relational self. It would be silly to call God as "primordial" the "Father." When we use such terms as Father, as Self-Expression or Word, and as Responsive Spirit we are applying them, or we ought to be doing so, to the whole concrete actuality of God as he is related to the creation, known to his creatures in many and various ways, and always concerned with them in his love, the Love which indeed he *is*.

For exactly the same reasons it would be silly to identify Word or Spirit specifically with the "consequent" aspect of deity. This is the accepted Process Thought term for God in his concrete actuality as affected by and in consequence as acting in the world. To call this "consequent" has its first meaning, of course, in that its reference is to God as the one who receives or accepts into himself that which the world accomplishes as it responds to his lure or attraction and by its own decision in freedom shapes what it is to become. This is true of every occasion, of every society of occasions, and of every human existence. But having thus accepted or received what the creation has to contribute, God harmonizes this with his own aim or purpose and then, so to say, plunges back into creation with the additional potentialities which are now available to him. I believe that we have here a formal and rather abstract way of saying exactly what biblical material says about God's whole relationship with the world, his respect for it, his lure exercised within it, his openness to influence by it, and his adaptation to it—and all this because he loves the creatures and both wills and works for their greatest fulfillment.

Once more, however, what is indicated by talk of Word as outgoing and operative with and alongside the world, and Spirit as responsive, operative in and through the world, can both be attributed to God in his "consequent" aspect, or in his concrete actuality. Therefore it does not readily make sense to assign specifically to these two "aspects" of deity, in Process ways of thinking, any of the three modes of divine existence and activity about which triunitarian thought would speak.

Even the sort of identification of the Spirit, in Cobb's fashion, with "particular providence" must be made with care, lest it imply some such precise correspondence of God's mode as Spirit with some particular element or category in the total Process scheme. To my mind this is not the proper procedure. I have accepted the point of Cobb's quasi-identification; but I am not prepared to go beyond seeing this as a way of talking about a particular and a general responsive movement through creation, in the Christian experience of answering faith and discipleship and also in a wider response anywhere and everywhere in the world. The "heightening and perfecting" which the Spirit accomplishes is exactly the consequence of the response made in the Spirit; and the importance of the use of those two words, "heightening" and "perfecting," is to be found in their pointing toward the results which God through his Spirit helps to bring about as he moves toward his world in lure and attraction, offering himself to be "prehended" through the many occasions which impinge on the creatures, and enabling their free answer to this prior movement toward them.

In essence, therefore, my contention is that the categories of Process Thought make available a way of seeing God as the active, living, related, and loving deity who is both chief causative agency and chief recipient. Process Thought will not provide us, however, with a set of terms or even with the necessary categories among which we may distribute the modes of existence and activity about which triunitarian doctrine speaks. What it *will* do is to make possible a general view of the world into which those modes may fit, if they are indeed as much part of the totality of Christian understanding in faith as I am convinced they must be. That ought to be sufficient, just as it is demonstrably helpful.

When Augustine used, as was necessary for him, the neo-Platonic world-view with which he was familiar, he did not cut his Christian convictions to fit that view. Or when and as he did this, it was unintentionally and unconsciously. At a later age, when Thomas Aquinas employed the Aristotelian categories which had been recovered just before and during his lifetime, he did not wish to modify the faith which he had received so that this faith would be explicitly "Aristotelian." Indeed, in the answers which he made to objections, he frequently insisted upon what he styled as "distinctions" in the senses in which words, and the concepts to which these words pointed, were being employed. Often he rejected what might have seemed the logically necessary "Aristotelian" consequences, in order to maintain what to him were the religiously necessary affirmations of the inherited faith. And if and when he did alter emphases in that faith, this was done without his intention but simply as a result of his inability to escape from the conceptuality which he employed.

I believe that those of us who wish to use the categories of Process Thought are in much the same position. But there is one highly important difference. Since we do not assume that Process Thought is utterly irreformable or think for a moment that it is the absolute truth, we are not so likely to fall into those unintentional and unconscious modifications of the deliverances of faith. Our task, as I see it, is to maintain the fundamental affirmations drawn from the abiding Christian experience, in all its variety yet with its overarching unity. This means that we are Christian believers, first, last, and always; and that our adoption of the Process conceptuality does not require us to become Whiteheadian, or any other kind of, scholastics who are determined to force everything into the Procrustean bed of some supposedly all-encompassing "system." We are *using* the insights of Process Thought; we are not its slaves. It is just here that I find some of my friends who, like me, are glad to be called "Process theologians" making a very grave mistake.

The Process view of the world does not offer us the exact details which Christian faith would affirm in respect to the distinctions in God's existence and relationship with the world. But neither does it rule out and render impossible our own acceptance of those distinctions and our own insistence that they can be "fitted into" the more general world-view which it proposes to us. The necessity is imposed upon contemporary Christian theologians to say that in his relationship with the creation God is indeed operative in the modes to which I have referred, while in his own existence those modes have some abiding counterpart in the unity of deity. Thus we wish to speak of God as the everlastingly creative agency who works anywhere and everywhere, yet without denying the reality of creaturely freedom—hence we point toward God as Parent. We wish also to speak of God as so working that he acts with and besides his creation, by luring it and attracting it toward realizing its possibilities and thereby achieving the fulfillment or satisfaction which is its aim—hence we point toward God as Self-Expressive Word. And we wish finally to speak of God as active in and through his creation in its accepting or "prehending" the lure or attraction which is offered to it, and thereby perfecting and heightening the intensity of its life and achieving fulfillment or satisfaction through a response which is richer and more adequate than the possibilities available through creaturely action alone—hence we point toward God as the Responsive Agency who is the Holy Spirit.

If then this entails some stretching of the categories of Process Thought, so be it. Whitehead himself was accustomed to say that his "system" as a system was open to modification in the light of other and further data. He never assumed that his "vision of reality" was conclusive and exhaustive; on the contrary, he was prepared to accept the possibility of addition and of what I have just styled "stretching" although he did not (so far as I am aware) use that last word. Charles Hartshorne, who is no "orthodox" Christian thinker, has yet been able to find in the traditional triunitarian position an insight into the richness of the divine nature and some indication of the way in which social as well as personal values are grounded in God. I am encouraged, by Whitehead's openness and by Hartshorne's affirmation of the validity of the insight present in the triunitarian position (although of course without any concern on his part for the detailed working-out of its implications), to believe that the argument of this book and especially of this chapter has validity. I hope that others will wish to pursue the matter and give us, in due time, a triunitarian doctrine which is more adequately developed, within the general world-view of Process Thought, than my own suggestions may have provided.

In the chapters of this book I have sought to give some of the reasons that many of us who are greatly concerned for a reconceiving of theology are convinced that there is genuine insight (as Professor Webb put it) in the ancient triunitarian doctrine; I have endeavored to make clear why we are not prepared to jettison it, like a piece of worn-out clothing or old luggage, simply because it has raised problems and in any event is not easy to understand in its usual conventional presentation. The reality of God, the supremely worshipful one who gives to his human creatures both "comradeship and refreshment," in Whitehead's words, is the central religious assertion. His activity in the world, everywhere found but focused in the event we call Jesus Christ, and his enhancing and enriching of life by its response to that universal and that particular activity: this is what Christian faith is all about. For us the doctrine of the divine triunity not only provides deep insight; it also gives a motive for adoring the mystery we name God.

How then may we put it, in conclusion? Perhaps like this. The belief that God is triune maintains for us the wonder and glory of the divine, guarantees for us that both personality and sociality are grounded in the way things go in the world, and opens to our minds and hearts the cosmic Love which creates us, which discloses itself to us, and which through our own response (however imperfect and feeble) enriches our lives—and adds joy to the being of God himself. *Himself:* for the cosmic Love is more suitably styled the cosmic Lover, the personalized and personalizing one who is making us "to move towards him, so that our hearts are unquiet until they find their rest in that movement towards God."

For Further Reading

Theologians using the Process conceptuality have for some time been working on a reconception of Christian thought, more particularly in the United States. But up to the present, little or no attention has been given to the doctrine of the divine Triunity; hence the present book.

The reader may be interested in following up the way in which these theologians have handled other major Christian doctrines. In respect to the doctrine of God, apart from consideration of his triunitarian nature, the most important contributions have been made by Charles Hartshorne, particularly in his *Man's Vision of God and the Logic of Theism* (Hamden, Conn.: Archon Books, 1964); *The Divine Relativity* (New Haven, Conn.: Yale University Press, 1948); *A Natural Theology for Our Time* (La Salle, Ill.: Open Court, 1967); *Reality as Social Process* (Boston: Beacon Press, 1953). Other books which should be mentioned are John B. Cobb's *A Christian Natural Theology* (London: Lutterworth, 1966) and *God and the World* (Philadelphia: Westminster Press, 1969); Ralph E. James's *The Concrete God* (Indianapolis: Bobbs-Merrill, 1967); and Schubert M. Ogden's *The Reality of God* (London: SCM Press, 1966). Peter N. Hamilton's *The Living God and the Modern World* (London: Hodder and Stoughton, 1967; Philadelphia: United Church Press, 1967) should also be noted.

In christological discussion my own *The Word Incarnate* (Digswell Place, Welwyn: Nisbet, 1959) was the first exploration in terms of Process Thought, with a further discussion in *Christology Reconsidered* (London: SCM Press, 1970). David Griffin's *A Process Christology* (Philadelphia: Westminster Press, 1974) is a valuable contribution to christological thought which deserves the most serious attention. In the treatment of the doctrine of the Holy Spirit, my *The Holy Spirit* (Philadelphia: United Church Press, 1974) is, to my knowledge, the only full-length book, although several essays have appeared from Process thinkers in learned theological journals. On the doctrine of the church, Bernard M. Lee's recent work *The Becoming of the Church* (Paramus, N.J.: Paulist-Newman Press, 1973) and my *The Christian Church as Social Process* (London: Epworth Press, 1971) may be mentioned.

Other doctrines or aspects of Christian thought (e.g., Atonement, the eschatological perspective, the nature of man) have been discussed in several books, the most notable of which is Daniel D. Williams' *The Spirit and the Forms of Love* (Digswell Place, Welwyn: Nisbet, 1968); this book has been called by Professor Cobb "a systematic theology in process terms" and without doubt is the most adequate survey of the whole field, with special stress upon the centrality of love in the Christian faith and hence in the theological formulation of that faith. Professor Williams' death in 1973 has deprived the theological world of further contributions which he had in mind, dealing with the doctrine of God, human nature, sexuality, and other subjects.